THE BIG BOOK OF JOKES & RIDDLES

Kidsbooks®

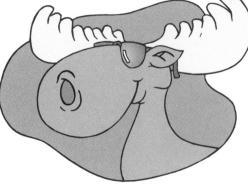

Copyright © 2006, 2010 Kidsbooks, LLC
3535 West Peterson Avenue
Chicago, IL 60659

All rights reserved including the right
of reproduction in whole or in part in any form.

Printed in the United States of America
091010003OH

Visit us at **www.kidsbooks.com**®

INTRODUCTION

What's more fun than a barrel of monkeys? A great big book of jokes and riddles, of course! If you love to snicker, giggle, chortle, chuckle, tehee, yuk it up, hee-haw, or guffaw, we have the laugh lines you're looking for.

Pick a page, any page, and see what you'll find: animal crack-ups, teacher/school send-ups, and cafeteria cutups—not to mention knock-knock jokes, sports quips, silly spy hijinks, wizard gags, and lots of other stuff that's just plain goofy.

If you're ready to tickle your funny bone—or someone else's—what are you waiting for? Turn the page and hop right into some humor!

HIC HIC

XTREME-LY FUNNY

Why don't snowboarders make good plumbers?

Because they only know about half-pipes!

What do you call the biggest skateboarder in the world?

Ollie-phant!

Why are skateboarders so cheap about buying clothes?

Because they believe in free style!

Why did the extreme surfer think that the sea was his friend?

Because it gave him a big wave as he went by!

Knock, knock!
Who's there?
Caddy!
Caddy who?
Caddy ya own surfboard, dude!

What is a bungee jumper's favorite part of a song?

The bridge!

What is a snowboarder's favorite type of vegetation?

The hand plant!

How do snowboarders face a hill?

Nose first!

What did the gloomy snowboarder say when he got off the lift?

"It's all downhill from here!"

Why are in-line skaters so excited?

Because they never feel board!

What did the boarders call the girl who loved to do 360s?

Mary-Go-Round!

What did the extreme biker call her winter wheels?

Her ice cycle!

Why did the skydiver feel a little nervous during her jump?

Because she had a sinking feeling!

What advice did the white-water kayaker give as he went over the rapid?

"Roll with it!"

Why did the skateboarder pick up speed going downhill?

Because he had an inclination to go faster!

What do you call the guy who is the world's best on the half-pipe?

The chairman of the board!

KNOCK, KNOCK!

Knock, knock!
Who's there?
Ben.
Ben Who?
*Ben a long time since
I've seen you!*

Knock, knock!
Who's there?
Don.
Don who?
*Don tell me you don't
remember me!*

Knock, knock!
Who's there?
Ax.
Ax who?
Ax nicely, and I might tell you!

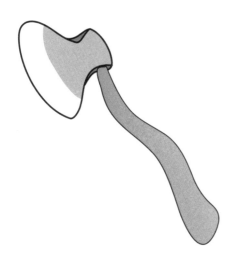

Knock, knock!
Who's there?
House!
House who?
*House about you let me
come inside?*

Knock, knock!
Who's there?
Arnold.
Arnold who?
Arnold friend from far away!

Knock, knock!
Who's there?
Isaiah!
Isaiah who?
*Isaiah nothing else until you
let me in!*

Knock, knock!
Who's there?
Osborn!
Osborn who?
Osborn today!
That makes it my birthday!

Knock, knock!
Who's there?
Chester!
Chester who?
Chester luck, you forgot
my name again!

Knock, knock!
Who's there?
Betty!
Betty who?
Betty doesn't even know
his own name!

Knock, knock!
Who's there?
Chuck!
Chuck who?
Chuck and see if you
recognize me!

Knock, knock!
Who's there?
Leggo!
Leggo who?
Leggo of me and I'll tell you!

Knock, knock!
Who's there?
Sultan!
Sultan who?
Sultan pepper makes everything
taste better!

RUBBER CHICKEN JOKES

Who tells the best rubber chicken jokes?

Comedi-HENS!

How does a rubber chicken send mail?

In a HEN-velope!

What do you get when you cross a rubber chicken with a cow?

ROOST beef!

Why did the rubber chicken cross the playground?

To get to the other SLIDE!

What do you get when you cross a rubber chicken with a cement mixer?

A bricklayer!

What do rubber chickens grow on?

Eggplants!

Why did the rubber chicken cross the road?
To get to the RUBBER side!
Why did the gum cross the road?
It was stuck to the chicken's foot!

Why did the turkey cross the road?

To prove he wasn't a chicken!

Why do rubber chickens make great basketball players?

Because they always bounce back in the fourth quarter!

Why is a fish easier to weigh than a rubber chicken?

Fish come with their own scales!

Why did the rubber chicken cross the basketball court?

He heard the referee calling FOWLS!

How does a rubber chicken make cake?

From scratch!

How did the rubber chicken learn to lay eggs?

The farmer showed him an EGG-xample!

Why couldn't the rubber chicken fly through the window?

It was closed!

When is the best time to buy rubber chicks?

When they're going CHEEP!

Why do rubber chickens lay eggs?

Because if they just dropped them, they'd break!

SILLY JOKES

What goes zzub, zzub, zzub?

A bee flying backward!

How do you catch monkeys?

Hang from a tree and make a noise like a banana!

Why can you dive from 300 feet right into a soda pop without hurting yourself?

Because it is a soft drink!

What happens when you cross an ape man with a tiger?

You get Tarzan stripes forever!

What do you use to cut through giant waves?

A sea saw!

Where do frogs leave their hats?

In a croakroom!

What do you get from nervous cows?

Milk shakes!

What do the animals read in zoos?

Gnuspapers!

What do you call pigs that write letters?

Pen pals!

What is green, curly, and plays pop music?

A transistor lettuce!

Which fish wears spurs and a cowboy hat?

Billy the Cod!

How would you describe a wild party at a camping site?

Intense (in tents) excitement!

Why didn't the two worms go into Noah's ark in an apple?

Because everyone had to go in pears!

What did the bull sing to the cow?

"When I fall in love, it will be for heifer."

Heard about the exhausted kangaroo?

He was out of bounds!

Wacky Wizardry

What do math wizards say when they lift a curse?

"Hex-a-gone!"

☆ 🌙 ☆

What did the wizard say when he couldn't find his wife?

"Witch way did she go?"

☆ ☀ ☆

If three ghosts run a race, which ghost will win?

The one with the most spirit!

☆ 🌙 ☆

What does a wizard's cat like just before it goes to bed?

A sorcerer of milk!

What did the wizard say when he met the witch he was going to marry?

"So, this is the bride and broom!"

☆ ☀ ☆

What does the wizard's sister eat when she goes to the beach?

Sand-witches!

☆ 🌙 ☆

What did the wizard's wife say when he changed her into a bird?

"Owl fly away!"

What is the favorite name for werewolves?

Harry! (hairy)

Why are wizards so good in fishing school?

Because they really know how to cast a spell!

☆ ☀ ☆

When the wizard found his friend, what had she been doing?

Witch-hiking!

☆ ☾ ☆

What did the wizard tell his wife after he tried to change her into a bird?

I've got some bat news . . . !

☆ ☀ ☆

What is the wizard's favorite soap opera called?

All My Cauldrons!

☆ ☀ ☆

What did the witch say to the monster that ate too fast?

"Wow, you really are a-gobblin'!"

☆ ☾ ☆

How does a wizard keep his potions safe from burglars?

With a warlock!

☆ ☀ ☆

What does a wizard say when he wants the lights to go on?

"Abra-candelabra!"

☆ ☾ ☆

Where do wizards go to test their skill?

Spelling bees!

SILLY SPIES

How do spies send secret messages in a forest?

By moss code!

What happened when the spy slept under the car?

She woke up oily the next morning!

What is a silly secret agent's favorite movie?

Spy Hard!

What is a junior secret agent's favorite movie?

Spy Kids!

Why did the secret agent cross the road?

To catch the other spy!

Why do gophers make good spies?

Because they know how to dig for dirt!

Where do sick spies go?

The ho-spy-tal!

What do you call it when one cow spies on another?

A steak-out!

What is a spy's favorite TV show?

Hidden Camera!

How did the spy feel when he spilled fruit punch on himself?

Like he'd been caught red-handed!

What do double-crossing spies do on vacation?

They lie around!

Why do informers smell so bad?

Because they're always spilling the beans!

What did the secret agent give the suspicious double-crossing spy?

A lie-defector test!

Why do mummies make good spies?

Because they are good at keeping things under wraps!

CAFETERIA COMEDY

What soup is fresh in the cafeteria but still boring?

Chicken new-dull!

What do little kids get at the cafeteria in the afternoon?

A nap-snack!
(knapsack)

Here's a cafeteria recipe: Throw out the outside, cook the inside, eat the outside, throw out the inside. What's it for?

An ear of corn!

Why did the cook bake bread for the cafeteria?

Because he kneaded the dough!

What is the worst-tasting drink in the cafeteria?

Nas-tea!

Where does the cook shop for vegetables?

The stalk market!

How did the cup and saucer feel about the shoddy way they had been washed?

They thought it was dish-picable!

What dessert should you always eat sitting down?

Chair-ee pie!

What makes the cook sadder the skinnier it gets?

An onion!

How do school inspectors like their eggs?

Hard-boiled!

What do you call it when you can't have dessert until after lunch?

Choco-late!

What did the potatoes say after the big vote?

"The eyes have it!"

What do you call someone who works in the cafeteria fixing fruit?

A peach cobbler!

UNDER WHERE?

Knock, knock!
Who's there?
Irish.
Irish who?
Irish my underwear wasn't showing!

What did the pair of underwear say when it was making a toast?

"Bottoms up!"

What did the man say when he took out his thermal underwear for the winter?

"Long time, no seam!"

What did the woman do with her silky underwear?

She satin them!

Why are boxer shorts so sad?

Because they feel under-appreciated!

What kind of dessert can you eat in your underwear?

Shortbread!

What did the army shorts say to the boxer shorts?

"Brief me!"

What kind of briefs do cows wear?

Udderwear!

What kind of briefs does Thor wear?

Thunderpants!

What do you feel when you have to throw out an old pair of underwear?

Brief grief!

Why was the musician so embarrassed when his shorts fell down?

Because he thought the band had let him down!

What did the tank top say to the pair of long underwear?

"Let's keep this brief!"

What did the long underwear say to the tank top?

"Don't be short with me!"

What did the silk underwear say to the cotton briefs?

"Slip around, you might learn something!"

What did the cotton briefs say to the silk underwear?

"Man, you're smooth!"

What kind of boxer shorts do supervillains wear?

Underworld underwear!

Why did the cat sing all morning long?

He had tune-a-fish for breakfast!

What do you get from an Arctic cow?

Cold cream!

What do you use to count cows?

A cow-culator!

What do you give a sick pig?

Oink-ment!

What did the owl think when he lost his voice?

He didn't give a hoot!

Why do geese fly south for the winter?

It's too far to walk!

What do you call a sleeping bull?

A bulldozer!

What kind of bird is always out of breath?

A puffin!

Why do fish live in salt water?

Because pepper makes them sneeze!

What do you get when you cross two elephants with a fish?

Swimming trunks!

Why are fish the smartest animals?

They spend all their time in a school!

Why did the farmer name his pig "Ink?"

Because it kept running out of the pen!

Why did the cow cross the road?

To get to the udder side!

If apes live in trees, where do they sleep?

In apricots!

Why are bison such good musicians?

They have fantastic horns!

CLASSROOM Crack-ups

What did the boy say when he had to clean the blackboards after class?

"I chalked it up to experience!"

What did the girl say when asked how her history class was?

"It's old hat!"

How long does history class feel?

"Four score and seven years . . ."

Why did the girl think that she was in charge of the class?

Because she had the ruler!

Why did the student mail a clock to his science class?

He wanted to see time travel!

What do you call a boy who excels in phys. ed.?

Jim! (gym)

What do you call a student who misses Spanish, French, and English classes?

Truant in three languages!

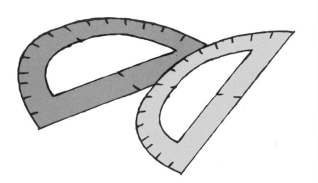

Why does math class feel so long?

It must be the protractors!

What did the boy who wanted to stay home say when asked where he didn't feel well?

"In school, mostly!"

What did the girl say when asked why she didn't like going to school?

"Oh, I like going. I just don't like getting there!"

Why did the student think that she could make toast in science class?

She heard that they'd be using bun-sun burners!
(Bunsen burners)

What is the best thing to eat in math class?

Pi!

What do you call the last day of school?

The first day of the year!

How do you know that you've been staring at the chalk too long?

When you get really board!

SILLY SPIES

What do you call a secret agent with great vision?

An eye spy!

Why did the spy spend the day in bed?

Because he was told to stay undercover!

What game do young spies learn on the playground?

Hide-and-seek!

What kind of food do super-sleuths love?

Spy-see food!

What is a secret agent's favorite car game?

I Spy!

What do you call a secret agent who spies for both sides?

Double trouble!

Why was Quasimodo such a good secret agent?

Because he always had a hunch!

What kind of shoes do athletic spies wear?

Sneak-ers!

Why did the spy think that something was wrong?

Because she had a sneaking suspicion!

How did the spy pass a test in spy school?

He cheated without getting caught!

What does the British Secret Service call its yellow-haired spy?

James Blond!

Why should you never play hide-and-seek with spies?

Because they always sneak a peek!

What is a spy's favorite dessert?

S-pie!

Why did the spy think that the floor had lips?

Because she knew that the walls had ears!

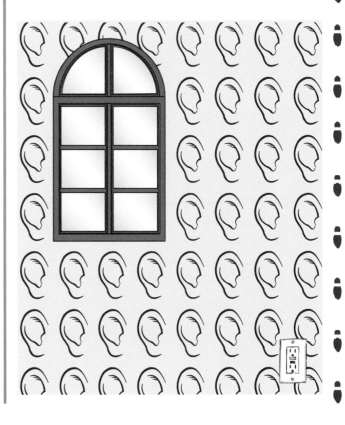

Every time Bob and Steve played hockey in Steve's driveway, Steve's dog would jump up and start biting Bob's leg.

One day, Bob asked Steve, "Is your dog trying to protect you from me?"

"No," replied Steve. "He just doesn't like hockey."

"He doesn't?" asked Bob. "How come?"

"Because," answered Steve. *"He's a boxer."*

Why didn't the puck go to jail?

Because the goalie saved him!

Fred: Did you hear about the center who stepped out of the shower soaking wet and turned on the light?
Jill: No, what happened?
Fred: *He took a penalty shock!*

Jill: Did you hear about the two players who were in the NHL even though they were only 15?
Fred: No, what happened?
Jill: *When the league found out, they got a double minor!*

Why was Cinderella's hockey team so bad?

She had a pumpkin for a coach!

What happened when the hockey player told a joke?

The ice cracked up!

What happened at the tie game when the ice melted?

The game went into sodden-depth overtime!

Why do the Halifax Hens have such bad uniforms?

Because they're cheep!

What is the hockey player's favorite part of cake?

The ICING, of course!

What do you get when you cross hockey skates with a bicycle?

An ice-cycle!

What part of a hockey arena is never the same?

The changing rooms!

Why are hockey players such bad dancers?

They're afraid of getting holding penalties!

How are defensemen like dentists?

They both take out teeth when they go to work.

UNDER WHERE?

How did the boxer feel when he ran out of underpants?

Short-tempered!

What kind of underwear works best for small dogs?

Boxer shorts, of course!

Knock, knock!
Who's there?
Lucy!
Lucy who?
Lucy lastic will make your underwear fall down!

What did the man say when he took off his too-tight underwear?

"That's a brief relief!"

Did you read the book about the history of underwear?

Yes, but I thought it was a little brief!

What do you call your evening underwear?

Late bloomers!

What do you see under there?

Underwear?

What do you call instructions for underwear?

The brief brief!

Why do underwear hate these kinds of books?

Because they're always the butt of the joke!

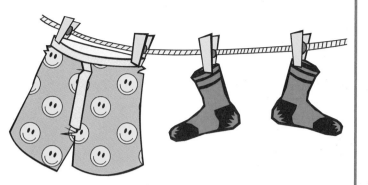

What did the boxer shorts say to the socks that were drying on the line?

"You hang out here often?"

What part of the military handles the underwear?

The rear admiralty!

Knock, knock!
Who's there?
Nunya!
Nunya who?
Nunya business what kind of boxer shorts I'm wearing!

What advice do you give to a contortionist about his underwear?

Don't get your shorts in a knot!

What did the man call the full-body underwear that he lost?

His long-gones!

How can your friends help you with your underwear in a pinch?

With a wedgie!

What do you call a man who forgets to put on his underpants?

Nicholas! (knicker-less)

XTREME-LY FUNNY

Why don't they build skate parks in outer space?

Because you can't get any air there!

What did the BMXer say when she crashed into the straw?

"I guess it's time to hit the hay!"

What do pro skateboarders love about their jobs?

The everyday grind!

What do you call a surfer who only wants to board in Rio?

Brazil nuts!

Knock, knock!
Who's there?
Canoe!
Canoe who?
Canoe help me wax my surfboard?

What do you call the best extreme skier?

Snow Wonder!

What do snowboarders do when they have an itch?

Pull a backscratcher!

What do BMXers love to do around Easter?

Bunny hops!

What happened when the BMXer landed the giant jump?

She got a big shock!

What do boarders love to do in public, even though it's bad manners?

The nosepick!

Why did the boarder think she could fly?

Because she was wearing her airwalks!

Why is in-line trick skating like flying a plane?

Because all anyone remembers is the landing!

Why don't Aussies get sleepy on the waves?

Because they're all wake boarding!

What do you say when an extreme rock climber almost falls?

"Get a grip!"

What did the boarder's friend say when she saw him wipe out?

"Looks like he's going to get that much-needed break!"

Why couldn't the silly man use his new water skis?

He was searching for a lake with a slope!

What is the most up-to-date animal in the zoo?

The gnu, of course!

What did the man say when he heard the story about the giraffe's hindquarters?

"Now that's a tall tail!"

Why are leopards easier to see than jaguars?

Because you can spot a leopard!

What kind of book is Black Beauty?

A pony tale!

What did the cheetah say when it was accused?

"You've gotta believe me! I'm not lion!"

Which big cat can you never trust?

The cheetah! (cheater)

What winged creature is the most sarcastic?

The mockingbird!

What type of bird is the most enthusiastic?

The ravin'!

What do housekeeper rodents do?

Mousework!

What did the antelope say when it read the paper?

"That's gnus to me!"

What school subject do snakes like best?

Hissssstory, of course!

What do frogs like best about vacationing in the tropics?

The croak-o-nuts!

What kind of shoes do frogs wear on vacation?

Open-toad sandals!

What do you call a snake that leads an orchestra?

A boa conductor!

SILLY JOKES

What is the most common illness among spies?

A code in the nose!

Who is Tibetan, hairy, and courageous?

Yak the Giant Hero!

What would you get if motorists were only allowed to drive pink minis?

A pink car nation!

Where do farmers leave their pigs when they go into town?

At porking meters!

Hear about the dancer who became a spy?

Her phone was tapped!

Who takes Christmas presents to police stations?

Santa Clues!

What is gray and has four legs and a trunk?

A mouse going on a holiday!

If buttercups are yellow, what color are hiccups?

Burple!

36

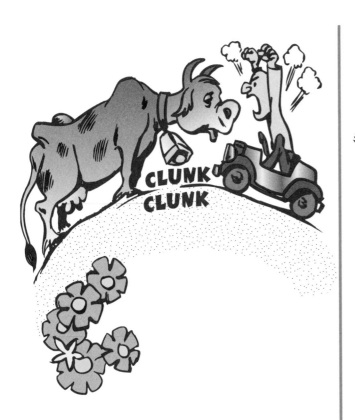

Why do cows wear bells?

Because their horns don't work!

What do you call an elf
that lives with your granny?

An old folk's gnome!

What is green, curly, and religious?

Lettuce pray!

Where do astronauts
leave their space ships?

At parking meteors!

What builds nests down in pits?

Mynah (miner) birds!

What do fish in the South Pacific sing?

"Salmon-chanted Evening"

What goes "Woof woof, tick tick"?

A watch dog!

Wacky Wizardry

What do you call a wizard who tells the weather?

A forecaster!

☆ ☾ ☆

What did the wizard name his daughter?

Wand-a!

☆ ☀ ☆

Why do wizards need housekeepers?

To take care of the magic dust!

☆ ☾ ☆

Why did the witch's children do so well in school?

Because they were wiz kids!

What do you call a phony wizard?

A magi-sham!

☆ ☀ ☆

What do you call a wizard with basic good manners?

Simply charming!

☆ ☾ ☆

Are all wizards good?

Not hex-actly!

☆ ☀ ☆

What do the young wizards call their oldest teacher?

Tyrannosaurus hex!

What did the little wizard say when his first spell worked?

"Hexellent!"

☆ ☀ ☆

Why don't single wizards dance?

Because they don't have ghoul-friends!

☆ ☽ ☆

What did the little wizards call their baseball team?

The Bat News Bears!

☆ ☀ ☆

What's a wizard's favorite subject in school?

Spelling!

☆ ☽ ☆

Why didn't the wizard predict the future for a living?

There was no prophet in it!

☆ ☀ ☆

What kind of jewelry do wizards wear?

Charm bracelets!

☆ ☽ ☆

Where do young wizards go to learn?

Charm school!

☆ ☽ ☆

How many wizards does it take to change a lightbulb?

None. Wizards don't need to use lightbulbs!

SILLY SPIES

What do spies give each other when they get married?

Decoder rings!

What did the American spy say when he had the proof?

"C I A-in't lying!"

Why did the spy handbook seem so empty?

Because it was written in invisible ink!

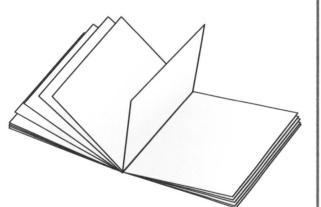

Who is a secret agent's favorite superhero?

Spy-derman!

What did the supervillain say to the spy?

"It isn't easy being mean!"

Who did the secret agent's reckless driver work for?

The Secret Swerve-ice!

Why did the spy say, "Keep your ear to the ground?"

Because he was listening for his shoe phone to ring!

What did the detective say to the handy spy?

"You're crafty!"

What does an undercover optometrist sell?

Spyglasses!

What do you call two spies in a diner?

Counter-espionage!

Why did the spy dig a hole in her backyard?

To hide her trench coat!

What villain is the most disagreeable?

Dr. No!

What do spies use to open secret doors?

A snea-key!

What did the spy discover about the laundered money?

It was a cover-up!

CAFETERIA COMEDY

Why did the student start a food fight with his meat loaf?

The only other option was to eat it!

What stops a cafeteria food fight?

A peas treaty!

What did the utensil say when the spoon asked what he was spooning?

"Try and fork-get about it!"

Why did the student not want to eat his mystery meat?

He wanted to have teeth left for dessert!

What do you call a cook at the cafeteria?

The torture king!

Why is the cook so funny at the cafeteria?

Because she'll have your stomach in knots!

What do you call someone who eats every bit of his cafeteria lunch?

A masochist!

When the cook was very angry, what did she do?

She whipped the cream!

Who loves the school cafeteria food?

My pet goat. But it also ate one of my shoes and a tin can for breakfast!

What is the one good reason to eat everything on your plate at the cafeteria today?

So it won't end up as leftovers tomorrow!

What do you call someone who volunteers to eat lunch at the school cafeteria?

Starving!

When is it okay to eat at a cafeteria?

When it is your last meal!

What does the sign over the cafeteria entrance say?

"Abandon all hope, ye who enter here!"

Why was the cook so mean to eggs?

He loved to beat them!

UNDER WHERE?

What do you call a telephone receptionist who wears silk boxer shorts?

A smooth operator!

What do you call bleached briefs that shrink in the wash?

Whitey tighties!

What kind of underwear do sheep wear?

Baaaaaxer shorts!

What do elephants wear to the beach?

Their swim trunks!

What kind of underwear do gardeners wear?

Bloomers!

What secrets do you hear about underwear?

Bloomer rumors!

What do you call scratchy woollen underwear?

Itchy britches!

What famous bear needs to wear diapers?

Winnie the Pooh!

What did the sign over the underwear store say?

"Get your butt in here!"

What does someone who makes underwear do?

He stitches britches!

Why did Santa need new underwear?

Because his were full of ho-ho-holes!

What did the nice woman say to the man in his swimming trunks?

"Those really suit you!"

Knock, knock!
Who's there?
Ican!
Ican who?
Ican see your underwear!

What did the vacationer say when he got too much sand in his swimsuit?

"I think I overpacked my trunks!"

What do you call someone who steals underwear from babies?

A diaper swiper!

XTREME-LY FUNNY

What did the experienced surfer say about the youngster who got stranded?

"Paddle teach him!"

Why do boarders love Thanksgiving?

It's a good chance to practice their carving!

What did the surfer think of the wave in front of him?

He thought it was swell!

Knock, knock!
Who's there?
Wanda!
Wanda who?
Wanda teach me how to snowboard?

What kind of music do surfers like best?

New wave, of course!

What dance do boarders go to every winter?

The Snowball!

Why do bikers get upset when they have to do the dishes?

Because they worry about their forks all the time!

What does a BMXer call his posse?

The Chain Gang!

What do you call a silly climber suspended on a rock face?

Dope on a rope!

What do you call a climber scrambling to keep her grip on the mountain?

Grope on a rope!

What do you call a climbing line hanging over a cliff?

Rope on a slope!

How did the climber get to the top of the mountain before everyone else?

He sneaked a peak!

Do most climbers think that they will fall?

Knot if they can help it!

What do climbers and plastic wrap have in common?

They both know how to cling on!

Why don't skydivers like portable phones?

Because they don't believe in going cordless!

What did the skydiver say when her pack didn't open?

"Chute!"

KNOCK, KNOCK!

Knock, knock!
Who's there?
Gino!
Gino who?
Gino who it is. I'm your twin brother!

Knock, knock!
Who's there?
Phil!
Phil who?
Phil my drink for me, will you?

Knock, knock!
Who's there?
Senior!
Senior who?
Senior so nosy, I'm not going to tell you who it is!

Knock, knock!
Who's there?
Leaf!
Leaf who?
Leaf me alone with all your silly questions!

Knock, knock!
Who's there?
Burton!
Burton who?
Burton me are going fishing, want to come?

Knock, knock!
Who's there?
Lion!
Lion who?
Lion down on the job will get you fired!

Knock, knock!
Who's there?
Iguana!
Iguana who?
Iguana hold your hand!

Knock, knock!
Who's there?
Hayden!
Hayden who?
Hayden won't do any good, I can see you through the mail slot!

Knock, knock!
Who's there?
Isis!
Isis who?
Isis giving me a brain freeze!

Knock, knock!
Who's there?
Izzy!
Izzy who?
Izzy coming out to play, or do I have to stand here all day?

Knock, knock!
Who's there?
Cello!
Cello who?
Cello there, my little friend. How are you?

Knock, knock!
Who's there?
Dennis!
Dennis who?
Dennis is my favorite game!

SILLY JOKES

What do you get when you cross a bell with a bee?

A humdinger!

What kind of ship did Dracula captain?

A blood vessel!

Who wears long underwear and glitters?

Long John Silver!

What did one toe say to the other toe?

"Don't look now, but there are a couple of heels following us!"

What moves around a bus at 1,000 mph?
A lightning conductor!

What do you do with a sick wasp?

Take it to the waspital!

What do you get when you pour hot water down rabbit holes?

Hot cross bunnies!

What is brown, hairy, and limps?

A coconut with blisters!

What do policemen say to men with three heads?

"Hello. Hello. Hello!"

What shows do ghosts like best at the theater?

Phantomines!

Who was Noah's wife?

Joan of Ark!

Why was the sheep arrested on the highway?

It made a ewe turn!

What is brown, has four legs, and can see as well from either end?

A horse with its eyes shut!

What is the best cure for flat feet?

A foot pump!

What is a British scientist's favorite food?

Fission chips!

What is essential for deaf fishermen?

A herring aid!

What do little witches call art day at school?

Witch craft day!

☆ ☽ ☆

What was wrong with the forgetful wizard's memory?

It had a tendency to wand-er!

What did the wizard say to his girlfriend before the dance?

"My dear, you look wand-erful!"

☆ ☀ ☆

What dance did the wizard take the witch to?

The Crystal Ball!

What did the wizard say to the vampire when he knew he was wrong?

"Sorry, it was a mis-stake!"

☆ ☀ ☆

Why did the wizard send his friend an hourglass in the mail?

He wanted to see time travel!

☆ ☽ ☆

What did the wizard's friend say after he turned him into an antelope?

"That's gnus to me!"

☆ ☀ ☆

How do witches know how much money you have?

Because they know how to tell your fortune!

What do wizards use to
open haunted houses?

A spoooo-key!

Why do wizards love to eat at
family restaurants?

*Because they have the
biggest potions!*

Why don't wizards like to
cast spells on boats?

They get potion sickness!

Why was the little wizard angry
at his big sister?

**Because she was always
potion him around!**

What did the old wizard say to his
frustrated pupil?

*"Stay calm, my son.
Potions is a virtue!"*

Why don't wizards need glasses?

Because they have eye of newt!

What did the wizard say to the spirit of
the gambling man?

*"You don't have a ghost
of a chance!"*

Why are ghosts vegetarians?

**Because they don't like to
haunt animals!**

What do you call a bear with no shoes?

Bear-foot!

What do you call a duck that steals?

A robber ducky!

What did the mother kangaroo give birth to?

A bouncing baby!

What do you call the place where desert animals rest?

Camel lot!

What can you call a camel without a hump?

Humphrey! (hump-free)

Why do tigers eat raw meat?

Because they're bad cooks!

What does a skunk buy for its home-entertainment system?

Smell-o-vision!

Why are skunks so dumb?

They never use good scents!

What do you call a monkey that has just turned seven?

A birthday baboon! (balloon)

Why do wolves have fur coats?

Because they would be cold wearing just hats!

What monkey is a real pal?

A chum-panzee!

How do you stop a wild boar from charging?

Take away its credit card!

What kind of bike does a polar bear ride?

An ice-cycle!

Why are elephants so cheap?

The get paid peanuts!

UNDER WHERE?

What kind of underwear does Muhammad Ali wear?

Boxers, of course!

What kind of swimsuits do pelicans wear?

Beak-inies!

What did the swimmer say about the little bikini?

"It was itsy-bitsy teenie-weenie!"

How did the woman in the swimsuit feel after escaping from a shark?

She felt lucky to be in a one-piece!

What do you call the money you use to buy underwear?

Shortbread!

What is the fastest swimsuit around?

The Speedo!

What did the sunbather have after falling asleep in his Speedo?

Hot crossed buns!

Why did the fast swimmer have to pull out of the race?

He got pulled over for Speedo-ing!

What kind of underwear do New York basketball players wear?

Knick-ers!

What did the woman call her fun, fancy underwear?

Her silly frillies!

What kind of underwear do baseball players wear?

Short stops!

Knock, knock!
Who's there?
C-2!
C-2 who?
C-2 it that you don't forget to wear your underwear!

What do you call old underwear?

Behind the times!

What do you call a snake that wears diapers?

A diaper viper!

Why won't Ron wear white underwear?

Because you can't white a Ron!

Where do you keep your shorts when you travel?

In your briefcase!

XTREME-LY FUNNY

Why do snowboarders make such bad farmers?

Because they hate to bale! (bail)

How do the snorkelers know when it's dinnertime?

They hear the diving bell!

What do divers use to take photos under the water?

A fish-eye lens, of course!

Why did the surfer cross the water?

To get to the other tide!

What was the saddest animal the diver had ever seen?

The blue whale!

What do skaters like that boxers hate?

A fat lip!

What does one wear to a surfer's wedding?

A good wet suit!

What kind of music do deep-sea divers love?

Sole music!

When should you never let a BMXer stay over at your house?

When she asks if she can crash on your couch!

What is a BMXer's worst enemy?

Gravity!

Why are boarders such dreamers?

Because they never want to come back down to earth!

What is the worst thing you can say to an in-line trick skater?

"You're grounded!"

What do skaters have in common with Fred Flintstone?

They all like to go bowling!

Knock, knock!
Who's there?
Indy!
Indy who?
Indy mood to go surfing?

What is it called when a wave is so big that a surfer doesn't stop until he hits the grass?

Surf and turf!

Why are surfers great gamblers?

Because they know when to let it ride!

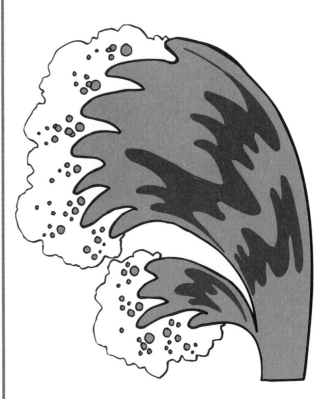

What fruit question is on the cafeteria menu?

What are melons? (watermelons)

What is the sad result of crossing a fruit with a dog?

Melon-collie!

What kind of fruit did the cook use to fix her flat tire?

A pump-kin!

How is holding a kind of rock just like a kind of fruit?

When you palm a granite! (pomegranate)

How did the cheese feel after the cook shredded it?

It was grate-full!

Where do baby cows go to eat lunch?

The calf-a-teria!

Where do cafeteria cooks go to prepare the potatoes?

To the mush-room!

What is golden soup made of?

Fourteen carrots! (carats)

What is a tree's favorite soft drink?

Root beer!

What did the cook say to a sulky grape?

"Quit your wining!"

What vegetable's easiest recipe is the same as its name?

Squash!

What is the opposite of spaghetti?

Antipasto!

What is the worst thing about eating in the cafeteria?

The food, of course!

Who loves cafeteria food?

Bugs!

SILLY SPIES

What is a young spy's favorite TV show?

Blue's Clues!

What did the spy say when his canine companion defected?

"Dog-gone it!"

What did the undercover agent name his dog?

Snoop-y!

Why was the sniffing spy dog so full of duty?

Because it knew what it had been scent to do!

Why did the secret agent think that his dog was a spy?

Because he caught it sniffing around!

What did the detective say to the spy dog?

"Please stop hounding me!"

What happened when the spy's dog lost the scent?

It got into a real furry flurry!

What did the spy dog say about sneaking around?

"It's a ruff job, but somebody's got to do it!"

What did the spy kitten want to be when it grew up?

A cat burglar!

Why did the spy dog like to be taken for a walk?

Because it knew that it would have a good lead!

Why do cats make good spies?

Because they know how to prowl!

What do you call the canine unit of the Secret Service?

The Federal Beagle of Investigation!

Where did the feline spy keep its gear?

In a tool kit-ten!

KNOCK, KNOCK!

Knock, knock!
Who's there?
Sara!
Sara who?
*Sara nother question
you could ask me?*

Knock, knock!
Who's there?
Ken!
Ken who?
*Ken I come in, or are you gonna
leave me out here all day?*

Knock, knock!
Who's there?
Ollie!
Ollie who?
*Ollie said was that I should
come visit you!*

Knock, knock!
Who's there?
Rufus!
Rufus who?
*Rufus leaking. You'd better
get it fixed!*

Knock, knock!
Who's there?
Don Juan!
Don Juan who?
*Don Juan to go to school today.
It's too nice outside!*

Knock, knock!
Who's there?
Shane!
Shane who?
Shane on you! You don't recognize your own brother!

Knock, knock!
Who's there?
Wade!
Wade who?
Wade till I get inside, then I'll tell you!

Knock, knock!
Who's there?
Tex!
Tex who?
Tex one to know one!

Knock, knock!
Who's there?
Lisa!
Lisa who?
Lisa you can do is let me in! It's pouring rain!

Knock, knock!
Who's there?
Simon!
Simon who?
Simon the other side of the door. If you opened it, you'd know!

Knock, knock!
Who's there?
Alfie!
Alfie who?
Alfie crying out loud, stop asking!

SILLY JOKES

What do nostalgic vampires sing?

"Fangs for the memory."

What would the Swiss be without all those mountains?

Alp-less!

Hear about the musical thief?

He got away with the lute!

How do you find out where a flea has bitten you?

You start from scratch!

What is wild, German, and lays eggs?

Attila the Hen!

Hear about the boxing canary?

He was a featherweight champion!

How about the author who made a fortune?

He was in the write business!

Who is a vampire's favorite composer?

Bathoven!

What is big, gray, and mutters?

A mumbo jumbo!

Why do devils and ghosts get along very well?

Because demons are a ghoul's best friend!

What happens when you cross a hen with a poodle?

You get pooched eggs!

How do you get through life with only one tooth?

You grin and bear it!

Why does Dracula love to go to the races?

He loves to bat on the horses!

What has four legs, is green, and is deadly when it jumps at you?

An angry billiard table!

Why do vampires brush their teeth regularly?

To avoid bat breath!

Wacky Wizardry

How do wizards guarantee peace?

They get a warlock!

What do little warlocks love on their nachos?

Cheese wiz!

Who is the most famous wiz of all?

Oz just about to ask you that!

What do wizards call phony spells?

Hocus bogus!

What did the wizard say after the fishing accident?

"Help! Hook-has poke-us!"

What do wizards say to their young students who can't concentrate?

"Hocus focus!"

What do you say to a wizard who is a daydreamer?

"Wish not, wand not!"

What does a wizard say when he gets to his front door?

"Open says me!"

What did the wizard say after he lost a game of chess to the little sprite?

"Fairy 'nuff!"

What did the wizard say to the lazy monster?

"Quit dragon your tail!"

⭐🌙⭐

What do wizards think of little, flying people?

That they're fairy interesting!

⭐☀️⭐

What did the wizard say to the little girl who wanted to study magic?

"Witching you the best of luck!"

⭐🌙⭐

Where did the wizard meet his elf friend for their fishing trip?

Down at the dwarf!

⭐☀️⭐

What did the wizard say when his little sidekick went away on vacation?

"I feel so elfless!"

⭐🌙⭐

Why can't babies do magic?

Because they don't know how to spell!

⭐☀️⭐

What did the wizard say when he was buying the elf's walking stick?

"Gnome your price!"

UNDER WHERE?

What kind of underwear do horses wear?

Jockeys!

What kind of jumps do jockeys do?

Girdle hurdles!

Why did the woman keep checking her pantyhose drawer?

Because she needed to take stocking!

What do you call it when Santa checks his inventory?

Christmas stocking!

What kind of socks do horn players wear?

Tuba socks!

What kind of underwear do comedians wear?

Joke-ys!

Why did the underwear keep moving around?

Because it was jockeying for position!

**What kind of underwear
fits over a shell?**

A turtle girdle!

**What did the boxer shorts
say to the pantyhose?**

"Sock it to me!"

**What kind of shirt do generals wear
under their suits?**

Tank tops, of course!

*Knock, knock!
Who's there?
Handel!
Handel who?
Handel your underwear
with care!*

**Where do pantyhose go
to meet stockings?**

To a sock hop!

How do you cover up your foot?

You socket!

**What do chickens wear
under their pants?**

Hen-derwear!

Why do stockings always feel safe?

*Because they've got a garter!
(guarder)*

**What kind of socks
do firefighters wear?**

Fire hose!

XTREME-LY FUNNY

How do you train for
the big wave?

Practice rip curls!

How do extreme surfers greet each
other?

Hey, Haw-ai-i?

What is the one hairstyle surfers
don't mind having?

A permanent wave!

What do extreme ski jumpers love
most about their car stereos?

The aerials!

Why were the surfers happy to hear
that a storm was coming?

*Because they thought it was a
wind-wind situation!*

Why didn't the man use his new
cross-country skis?

*He was searching for a very small
country!*

How did the reckless skier get rid of
her extra gear?

She had a yard sale!

Knock, knock!
Who's there?
Ida!
Ida who?
*Ida like to learn how to
ride a BMX bike!*

How did the extreme jumper show that he was excited?

He flipped out!

Why didn't the musician board on the big hill?

She was afraid that she'd B flat!

How did the bummed-out boarder pick himself up?

He got on the chair lift!

When you take the big jump, what are your rhyming choices mid-air?

Sail or bail!

Who won when the climbers raced to make the quickest knot?

It was a tie!

Why was the climbing movie split into two parts?

Because it was a cliff-hanger!

How did the surfer feel after a whole weekend on the sunny sea?

Burned out!

How did the diver's trip go?

Swimmingly!

KNOCK, KNOCK!

Knock, knock!
Who's there?
Little old lady!
Little old lady who?
I didn't know you could yodel!

Knock, knock!
Who's there?
Cassidy!
Cassidy who?
Cassidy was going to be right back.
Is he home?

Knock, knock!
Who's there?
Sam!
Sam who?
Sam day, you'll remember.

Knock, knock!
Who's there?
Zoe!
Zoe who?
Zoe doesn't recognize my voice now?

Knock, knock!
Who's there?
Maya!
Maya who?
Maya foot seems to be a caught in your door!

Knock, knock!
Who's there?
Yuri!
Yuri who?
Yuri up and open the door!

Knock, knock!
Who's there?
Mabel!
Mabel who?
Mabel syrup is good on waffles!

Knock, knock!
Who's there?
Ach!
Ach who?
Gesundheit!

Knock, knock!
Who's there?
Klaus!
Klaus who?
Klaus the window, I can hear your television all the way down the street!

Knock, knock!
Who's there?
Deecha!
Deecha who?
Deecha miss me while I was gone?

Knock, knock!
Who's there?
Thermos!
Thermos who?
Thermos be some way out of here!

Knock, knock!
Who's there?
Colleen!
Colleen who?
Colleen all cars! Colleen all cars! We have a knock-knock joke in progress!

SILLY SPIES

Why did the scuba-diving agent
feel so low?

Because she had a sinking feeling!

What happened to the
scuba-diving spy?

He tanked!

Why didn't the spy want to dive to
the sunken sub?

He couldn't handle the pressure!

What do deep-sea spies have
for lunch?

Subs!

Where was the scuba-diving spy
afraid to swim?

In the Dead Sea!

What did the spy find on the ship?

A conspira-sea!

Why didn't anybody believe the
scuba-diving spy?

*Because she had no ground to
stand on!*

Why did the scuba-diving spy hate it
when his phone rang under water?

Because it left a wringing in his ears!

What did the secret agent do when he got on board the boat?

He performed a ship-search!

What do you call an underwater secret agent?

James Pond!

Where do spies go when they die?

To double-oh-heaven!

How can spy submarines see so well?

Because they're made for deep-sea vision!

What should every sloppy spy have?

A license to spill!

What did the spy call the fishy dealer?

A card shark!

SILLY JOKES

What do you call a pig who tells long, dull stories?

A big boar, of course!

Why did the princess fall in love with the taxi?

Because it was a very handsome cab! (hansom cab)

What did the big flower say to the little flower?

"How are you, bud?"

Why was the baker so lazy?

He did nothing but loaf!

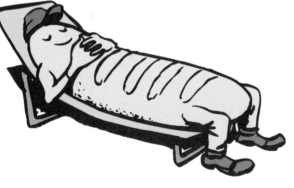

Why do elephants paint their toenails red?

So they can hide in cherry trees!

Why do people carry umbrellas?

Because umbrellas can't walk!

Why didn't the coffee cake have many friends?

It was crumby!

What was the baker's favorite dance?

The twist!

Why is the baker so rich?

He makes a lot of dough!

How do you get four elephants into a compact car?

Two in the front and two in the back!

How do you get four giraffes into the same compact car?

You can't until you get those elephants out!

Where do sugar fairies live?

Gnome sweet gnome!

What do you call a mischievous egg?

A practical yolk!

Who is short, afraid of wolves, and shouts a lot?

Little Rude Riding Hood!

What do you call a cat that sucks lemons?

A sour puss!

Who has huge antlers and wears white gloves?

Mickey Moose!

Wacky Wizardry

What do American fairies sing at the beginning of every baseball game?

Stars and Sprites!

⭐🌙⭐

Why do wizards make good friends?

Because they're charming!

⭐☀️⭐

How are wizards' books held together?

They're spellbound!

What is it called when wizards get together and sing without instruments?

Acca-spell-a! (a cappella)

Where do witches go when they run out of eye of newt and tongue of frog?

To the gross-ery store!

What do speedy monsters love to do most?

Dragon racing!

What did the elf say when he was tired of Oz?

"There's no place like gnome!"

☆ 🌙 ☆

Why do witches chew gum?

Because they're afraid of having bat breath!

☆ ☀ ☆

What do wizards call their magic books?

The Go-spell!

☆ 🌙 ☆

What is the name of the richest American wizard?

Rocka-spell-a! (Rockefeller)

☆ ☀ ☆

Why did the witch decide to get a new broom?

She wanted to make a clean sweep of it!

☆ 🌙 ☆

Why did the witch need to practice with her new broom?

Because she needed to brush up on her flying!

Why do witches fly to their secret caves?

Because it's too far to walk!

☆ ☀ ☆

What did the wizard's kitten say before his magic trick?

"Abra cat-abra!"

☆ 🌙 ☆

What did the pirate want the witch to find for him?

Sleeping booty!

☆ ☀ ☆

Knock, knock!
Who's there?
Witches!
Witches who?
Witches to put a spell on you!

CAFETERIA COMEDY

What do the geeks eat in the cafeteria?

Square meals!

Why should you go to the cafeteria before computer class?

To have a little byte!

Why did the boy swallow the dollar bill?

His parents told him it was his lunch money!

When are students like pigs?

When they eat the slop at the cafeteria!

What do you say when you find a dead bug in your soup at school?

"He must have tasted it!"

What did one cook say to the other when they went on vacation?

"Meat me in St. Louis!"

How do you know when it's time to eat at the cafeteria?

When they lock the doors behind you!

What did the student from France say after eating lunch at the cafeteria?

"Mercy!" (merci)

What is the difference between the school cafeteria's meat loaf and bricks?

Not much!

Why was the student looking at his lunch with a magnifying glass?

She was trying to solve the mystery meat!

What do you call something that is brown and sticky in your food at the cafeteria?

A stick!

When there is only one thing on the menu at school, how come you still have a choice?

You can choose not to eat it!

Why did the girl think that she had chicken pox?

Because the chicken she had at the cafeteria was a little spotty!

How do you know lunch is over at the cafeteria?

By all the moaning!

UNDER WHERE?

What do you call a shirt that Sir Lancelot wears to sleep?

A knight shirt!

What is a clean pair of stockings' favorite sports team?

The Chicago White Sox, of course!

Knock, knock!
Who's there?
Warren!
Warren who?
I'm Warren my favorite pair of underwear!

What do you call indoor shoes that help you slide?

House slippers!

What are the best initials for comfy sleeping?

P.J.!

What do you call bright yellow PJs?

Banana pajamas!

What do you call PJs that are too small?

Tighty nighties!

What kind of underwear does a home wear?

A housecoat!

What do you call shoes that you wear to bed?

Sleeper slippers!

What do you call a housecoat that you wear to make a salad?

A dressing gown!

What do you call women's shorts that are always behind?

Fanny!

What does the postman wear on his feet at night?

Shipper slippers!

What do you call it when you throw out the top of your underwear?

Waste-band! (waistband)

What do underwear like to read?

Boxer short stories!

What do you call it when you quickly alter your long underwear?

A short cut!

What does the green-thumbed woman wear on her legs?

Garden hose!

What did the in-line skater say after crashing down the hill?

"Give me a brake!"

Knock, knock!
Who's there?
Claire!
Claire who?
Claire the way, I'm coming down the hill!

What do you call an in-line skater who crashes and burns?

A trailblazer!

What part of the in-line skate can you never trust?

The heel!

How do you say good-bye to an in-line fanatic?

"Later, skater!"

What did the in-line skater say when she got lost in the skate shop?

"I can't seem to get my bearings!"

What is the in-line skater's motto?

Roll with it!

How did the boarder make the hill angry?

He just kept crossing it!

What did the in-line skater say to his buddy when he saw dogs chasing them?

"Don't look now, but I think we're being tailed!"

What is the worst part about racing downhill against the clock?

The time is always running down!

Why do in-line skates seem so rude?

Because they always stick out their tongues!

What do you get when you rewind your skate-tricks video?

Some wicked backslides!

What do boarders have in common with martial artists?

They both love the kick flip!

What do boarders have in common with the big rig riders?

They all love their trucks!

What did the boarders say when they were playing hide and seek?

"Ollie, Ollie, oxen free!"

What did the dentist say to the skater?

"I want you to stop grinding your teeth!"

KNOCK, KNOCK!

Knock, knock!
Who's there?
Boo!
Boo who?
There, there, don't cry.

Knock, knock!
Who's there?
Paul!
Paul who?
Paul up a chair, and I'll tell you!

Knock, knock!
Who's there?
Sandy!
Sandy who?
Sandy beaches beat snowstorms any day!

Knock, knock!
Who's there?
Max!
Max who?
Max no difference if you let me in or not! I can wait all day!

Knock, knock!
Who's there?
Daryl!
Daryl who?
Daryl never be another girl like you!

Knock, knock!
Who's there?
Mary!
Mary who?
Mary me, why don't ya?

Knock, knock!
Who's there?
Tom Sawyer!
Tom Sawyer who?
Tom Sawyer paint job on his fence.
Boy are you in trouble!

Knock, knock!
Who's there?
Simon!
Simon who?
Simon the dotted line and all your
troubles will be over!

Knock, knock!
Who's there?
Water!
Water who?
Water you waiting for? Open up!

Knock, knock!
Who's there?
Tony!
Tony who?
Tony even know me anymore?

Knock, knock!
Who's there?
Sweden!
Sweden who?
Sweden sour chicken is yummy!

Knock, knock!
Who's there?
Augusta!
Augusta who?
Augusta wind is coming
your way!

SILLY JOKES

What goes "Dit-dit-dot bzzz" and
then bites you?

A morsequito!

Who wrote Great Eggspectations?

Charles Chickens!

What is bright yellow, weighs a ton,
has four legs, and sings?

Two half-ton canaries!

Why do bears have fur coats?

Because they would look silly
in raincoats!

What do ghosts have for breakfast?

Dreaded wheat!

Why do insects hum?

Because they don't know the words!

What do vampires take
for a bad cold?

Coffin drops!

What happens when you cross a Jeep
with a pet dog?

You get a land rover!

It's sad about the human cannonball
at the circus.

He got fired!

What animal hibernates standing on its head?

Yoga Bear!

What is green, knobby, and writes essays?

A ball-point pickle!

Hear about the burglars who stole a calendar?

They each got six months!

What did one raisin say to the other raisin?

Nothing. Raisins can't talk!

Who couldn't get their airplane to fly?

The wrong brothers!

What do you need to get back runaway rabbits?

Hare restorer!

Pet Punchlines

What do you get when you cross a cat and a fish?

A purr-anha!

Why shouldn't you keep a piranha as a pet?

Because it has a fish's temper!

How do cats stop their favorite videos?

They put them on paws! (pause)

What did the cat say after it caught the rat?

"Sorry, my mouse-stake!"

What kind of feline can you never trust?

A copycat!

What kind of dogs always get into fights?

Boxers!

What happened to the teddy bear that got into a fight with a dog?

He got the stuffing knocked out of him!

What kind of pet always has a sore throat?

A hoarse!

What does your cat like on hot days?

Mice cubes!

How do you reward a horse that pulls your carriage on your wedding day?

With a bridle sweet!

What did one cat say to the other after it saw that they were being followed by a dog?

"Don't look now, but I think we're being tailed!"

What do you feed a cat that yowls all night long?

Tune-a-fish!

Which dog makes the most boring pet?

The poo-dull!

Which side of a dog has the most hair?

The outside!

SILLY SPIES

What did the spy say to his friend who was hiding behind the curtain?

"Pull yourself together!"

What did the secret agent say to the camping spy?

"You're so tents!"

Why did the spy hate to play cards at the casino?

Because she found them hard to deal with!

Why did the detective think that snooping around an apple farm would help him solve the case?

He thought he would get to the core of it!

What did the spy say after she got poison ivy from spying in the bushes?

"I made a rash decision!"

What did the spy think about having to drill peepholes in a wall all day?

That it was really boring!

Why didn't the spy want to look for clues in the trash?

Because he thought it was a waste of time!

Why did the spy think the forgery ring was hilarious?

Because of all the funny money!

What did the martial-arts spy drink in the afternoon?

Kara-tea!

What did the spy think after he was bitten by mosquitoes in the swamp?

That he was a sucker for taking the job!

What did the spy say about his enemy who got out of the cheese factory?

"He made a grate escape!"

Why wasn't the spy surprised that his enemy wanted to lower him into boiling oil?

Because it was Fry-day!

How did the spy feel when the enemy agent stole his shoes?

De-feeted!

Why did the spy put a banana peel in front of his closet?

So he could slip into something more comfortable!

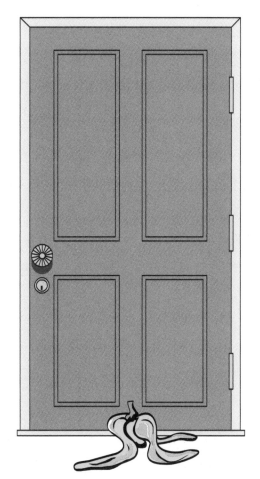

Wacky Wizardry

Knock, knock!
Who's there?
Wiz!
Wiz who?
Wiz a matter, you don't recognize me?

☆ ☽ ☆

If you spin around and around, what kind of magic will you create?

A dizzy spell!

☆ ☀ ☆

What kind of spell makes you thirsty?

A dry spell!

☆ ☽ ☆

What is a witch's favorite pet?

A wart hog!

☆ ☀ ☆

Who is a witch's favorite musician?

Bats Domino!

☆ ☽ ☆

What is a vampire's favorite sport?

Batsball!

Why are magicians such fast readers?

Because they know how to wiz through a good book!

☆ ☀ ☆

Why don't vampires change into pelicans?

Because pelicans are too big to fly in through bedroom windows!

☆ ☽ ☆

What is a wizard's favorite cereal?

Lucky Charms!

What do you call the most powerful wizard of all?

Whatever he wants you to!

☆) ☆

What do you call a female wizard at the beach?

A sandy-witch!

☆ ☀ ☆

What do you call a criminal elf?

A lepre-con!

☆) ☆

What do Eskimo leprechauns keep at the end of the rainbow?

A lucky pot of cold!

What do you call a leprechaun's dog?

A four-leafed Rover!

☆) ☆

What did the Bigfoot put in his garden?

Sas-squash!

☆ ☀ ☆

How do wizards roast their marshmallows?

With dragon's breath!

COMIC CRITTERS

What do you call a greasy pachyderm?

An oily-phant!

Why was Billy so mad?

Somebody got his goat!

How do rabbits toast each other?

"Hare's to you!"

What did the big buffalo say as the little buffalo left for school?

"Bison!" ("Bye, son!")

What is the best prison for a criminal deer?

Elk-a-traz! (Alcatraz)

Where do big cats go when they're sick?

To leopard (leper) colonies!

What do you call a battle between the big cats of the wild?

A jag war! (jaguar)

How do lions do their shopping?

From cat-alogues!

Why don't snakes need eating utensils?

Because they have forked tongues!

What do you call a rhino that's been injured?

A rhino-sore-us!

What is the cheapest animal to hire in the jungle?

An elephant—it will work for peanuts!

Why did the elk buy a set of weights?

To help build up his moose-els!

What is an orangutan's favorite tool?

A monkey wrench!

How did the lamb feel after being shorn?

A bit sheepish!

TEACHER TICKLERS

What did the student say when the teacher asked what he would have if he got $20 each from 10 people?

"A new skateboard!"

Teacher: **"When was there the most water on Earth?"**
Student: **"During the rain (reign) of Caesar?"**

Why did the teacher fail the student who got a hundred in math?

Because the answer was 40!

What is the saying about feeding the teacher?

An apple a day keeps summer school away!

Why wasn't the English teacher good at geometry?

He came at it from the wrong angle!

What did the teacher tell the student who incorrectly identified a bison?

"I'm sorry, that's a moose-take!"

What did the students think of their teacher's cheesy clothes?

They thought they were grate!

When the teacher asked the student why he had said that Rome was built at night, what did he say?

"Well, I know it wasn't built in a day!"

Why did the student ask her teacher if the early settlers were depressed?

Because they were called the pil-GRIMS!

What did the student tell his history teacher that the Vikings had invented?

Norse code!

How did the teacher finish the year?

In summery! (summary)

Why did the students call their teacher "The Moose"?

Because he wore horn-rimmed glasses!

What do history teachers make when they want to get together?

Dates!

What do history teachers talk about when they get together?

Old times!

UNDER WHERE?

What's a good nickname for little underwear?

Short stuff!

What do you call it when a baby wets its diaper?

Britches over troubled water!

What advice did the underwear give the man?

Don't wear me out!

Knock, knock!
Who's there?
Tom Sawyer!
Tom Sawyer who?
Tom Saw-yer underwear!

What do you call underwear with a picture of the night sky on it?

Fruit of the moons!

What kind of underwear does a giant wear?

Long johns!

What do you put on under your dress when you want to sneak out of a movie early?

A slip!

What do you call your most brightly colored boxers?

Your fundies!

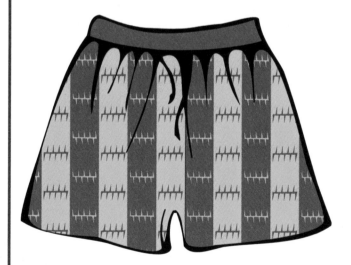

Why did everyone shun
the dark underwear?

*Because it was the black shorts
of the family!*

*Knock, knock!
Who's there?
Pam!
Pam who?
Pam-per that baby so she
doesn't wet herself!*

What do you call three pairs
of work socks?

A socket set!

What do you call boxer shorts
with only one leg?

Blunderwear!

Why did the man put his underwear
on before his striped pants?

He wanted to see it behind bars!

What do you call people who think
about how the back of their
underwear looks?

Hind-brained!

Why did the underwear want everyone
to see him being active?

*Because he didn't want people
to think he was bum-bling!*

Why did the underwear want to
sneak into the drawer unnoticed?

*Because it didn't want
any fanny-fare! (fanfare)*

Why do some skaters' faces look so nasty?

Because of their noseblunts!

Why did the BMXer have a shower halfway through the race?

He wanted to make a clean break!

Why are skaters so bummed out?

Because they're always doing the downhill slide!

Knock, knock!
Who's there?
Mick!
Mick who?
McTwist!

Why are boarders so good at division?

Because they always know what half a 360 is!

What is the worst part about falling on the steps when you're boarding?

Bailing on the railing!

Why do windsurfers hate pollution so much?

Because they love to get good air!

What did the first-time skier say about his first day on the slope?

"By the time I learned to stand up, I couldn't sit down!"

What did the hang glider say after his first run?

"That was pretty good for a first draft!"

Why do snowboarders hate to be at the back of a plane?

Because it's harder to catch frontside air!

Why are deep-sea divers so tense?

They're under a lot of pressure!

How do big-wave hunters learn the rules?

They go to the surfboard!

Where do surfers learn to dance?

On boogie boards!

What do Hawaiian surfers do when they're tired?

They lei down!

What did the shark say to the surfer when it chomped on her board?

"I just stopped by for a bite!"

What do surfers not mind breaking?

Waves!

KNOCK, KNOCK!

Knock, knock!
Who's there?
Noah!
Noah who?
*Noah don't recognize
your voice either!*

Knock, knock!
Who's there?
Deluxe!
Deluxe who?
Deluxe Ness Monster!

Knock, knock!
Who's there?
Kerry!
Kerry who?
*Kerry me upstairs, would you?
I'm pooped!*

Knock, knock!
Who's there?
Felix!
Felix who?
*Felix me again, I'm never petting
your dog again!*

Knock, knock!
Who's there?
Barry!
Barry who?
Barry happy to meet you!

Knock, knock!
Who's there?
Manny!
Manny who?
*Manny needs a bath, have you
smelled him?*

Knock, knock!
Who's there?
Ping-Pong!
Ping-Pong who?
Ping-Pong, the bells are ringing!

Knock, knock!
Who's there?
Fletcher!
Fletcher who?
Fletcher self relax a little. Let go
every once in a while!

Knock, knock!
Who's there?
Francis!
Francis who?
Francis hello and wants to know
what you're doing later.

Knock, knock!
Who's there?
Sammy
Sammy who?
Sammy the check in
the mail!

Knock, knock!
Who's there?
Tyson!
Tyson who?
Tyson sugar on your cereal.
It's good!

Knock, knock!
Who's there?
Ember!
Ember who?
Ember me? I'm your
best friend!

SILLY JOKES

What kind of music do witches
play on their pianos?

Hagtime!

Why are bananas not
growing any longer?

*Because they are
long enough already!*

Which detective takes bubble baths?

Sherlock Foams!

Why do only very small elves
live under toadstools?

Because there is not mushroom!

What bellows, "Eef if of muf"?

A backward giant!

What did they call kittens
in the Wild West?

Posse cats!

Why can't you send letters to
Washington anymore?

Because he's dead!

Why did the carpenter
get tired of his work?

He got board!

Why did the window say, "Ouch?"

It had a pane!

What is the best way to
avoid falling hair?

Jump out of the way!

What do you give bald rabbits?

Hare tonic!

Which play did Shakespeare write
for baby pigs?

Hamlet!

What do sad fir trees do?

They pine a lot!

What happens when you put snakes
on a car window?

You get windshield vipers!

What is Beethoven doing
in his coffin?

De-composing!

Wacky Wizardry

What do you call a sloppy magic creature in a pond?

The Loch Mess monster!

☆ ☽ ☆

What did the umpire say when the wizard was up to bat?

"Swing and a miss-tical!"

☆ ☀ ☆

Knock, knock!
Who's there?
Who!
Who who?
Hey, you must be the wizard's owl!

☆ ☽ ☆

What is the spell for keeping animals indoors?

Z-O-O!

☆ ☀ ☆

What color robe does the wizard's cat wear?

Purr-ple, of course!

Other than garlic, what is a vampire's least favorite food?

Stake!

☆ ☀ ☆

What do wizards wear when they get out of the bath?

Their magic robes!

☆ ☽ ☆

What did the wizard say when he had the television remote?

"Press-to change-o!"

☆ ☀ ☆

What is a wizard's favorite drink?

Witches' brew!

What did the wizard say to the reptile that surprised him?

"Hey you, don't snake up on me!"

☆ ☽ ☆

How did the wizard catch the big fish?

Tricka trout!

☆ ☀ ☆

What kind of seafood do gnomes like best?

Sh-elf fish!

☆ ☽ ☆

What kind of monsters spit the most?

Gob-lins!

☆ ☀ ☆

What kind of candy do goblins hate the most?

Gob-stoppers!

☆ ☽ ☆

What do you find in a monster's belly button?

Gob-lint!

☆ ☀ ☆

What do you call an elf with a green thumb?

A garden gnome!

UNDER WHERE?

What do you call it when you don't need to take your shorts to the cleaners?

Wash and underwear!

Knock, knock!
Who's there?
Underwear!
Underwear who?
Underwear my pants are!

What do you call your full-body Fruit of the Looms?

Your fruit suit!

Where do you wear the swimsuit that you've wanted to wear all year?

In the waiting pool!

What do you call the fast swimming style that your new bathing suit gives you?

A stroke of genius!

Where did the stylish new swimsuit put the racer?

In the fast lane!

Knock, knock!
Who's there?
Owen!
Owen who?
I Owen 10 pairs of boxer shorts!

Why did the cheap boxer shorts salesman do so well?

Because he under-cut the competition!

What kind of underwear do superheroines wear?

Wonderwear!

Why did the underwear feel so low?

Because they just bottomed out!

What do you call the most helpful socks?

Support hose!

What kind of boxers will you get for the holidays?

Yule have to wait to find out!

What do you call formal boxer shorts?

Butt-on downs!

What kind of movies do underpants love?

Boxer short films!

What do you call it when the lining of a dress gets tangled?

A slip knot!

How can you spot dancing underwear?

With polka dots!

SILLY SPIES

What did the spy say when someone asked, "Did I just see you snooping?"

"Gee, I hope not!"

Why did the spy wear two pairs of glasses?

Because he wanted to have four-sight!

What did the perfumed agent say to the spy?

"Did you get the secret message I scent?"

What did the spy hear on his shoe phone when he was put on hold?

Sole music!

Why was the sleuth spending so much time around the chicken coop?

Because she suspected fowl play!

What did she say when she found out that she was right?

"Aha! Eggs-actly as I thought!"

What do you call a spy movie set at the North Pole?

A chiller thriller!

How did the cowboy spy communicate with the home office?

By saddle-lite!

What did Sherlock Holmes say to his friend about a grade school for spies?

"It's elementary, my dear Watson!"

What do you call a spy with a runny nose?

A dribble agent!

What did the man say when he uncovered the slouching spy?

"Im-posture!"

What did the spy call the comedian double agent?

A funny phony!

What did the secret agent think about the time he spent spying on a rabbit farm?

That it was a hare-raising adventure!

Why do international spies always want to run the world?

Because they love jog-raphy!

XTREME-LY FUNNY

What does a mountain climber have in common with a map?

They both work to scale!

How did the mountain biker approach the hill?

He got all geared up about it!

What do mountain bikers call apartments where they stop to rest?

Their brake pads!

What do mountain bikers call the helmets that protect their heads?

Brain buckets!

What is the smelliest part of a mountain biking race?

De-scent!

What did the other racers call the team from Finland?

The Finnish line!

How do extreme mountain bikers feel about broken pedals?

A little cranky!

Why are trick riders so high-strung?

Because they're a little jumpy!

What type of vegetation do snowboarders hate?

Face plants!

How did the hang glider feel after sailing for an hour through a storm?

A little winded!

What did the rider get after doing the tough course in the rain?

An obsta-cold!

What did the mountain biker do after her bike collided with another bike tire?

They spoke about it for a while!

What do big-mountain snowboarders call December to February?

Peak season!

What do extreme bikers think of riding through bear country?

It's grizzly!

Where do mountain bikers look for classifieds?

In the ad-venture!

Knock, knock!
Who's there?
Al!
Al who?
Al-pine skiing!

KNOCK, KNOCK!

Knock, knock!
Who's there?
You!
You who?
Yes, how can I help you?

Knock, knock!
Who's there?
Liam!
Liam who?
**Liam where he is. If he wants
to come, he'll come!**

Knock, knock!
Who's there?
Les!
Les who?
*Les go swimming
while it's still sunny!*

Knock, knock!
Who's there?
Fred!
Fred who?
Fred Sox are my favorite team!

Knock, knock!
Who's there?
Fuschia!
Fuschia who?
*Fuschia the door on me
one more time, that's it!*

Knock, knock!
Who's there?
Vaughn!
Vaughn who?
**Vaughn day you'll stop
acting so crazy!**

Knock, knock!
Who's there?
Theodore!
Theodore who?
*Theodore is locked! Come in
this one instead.*

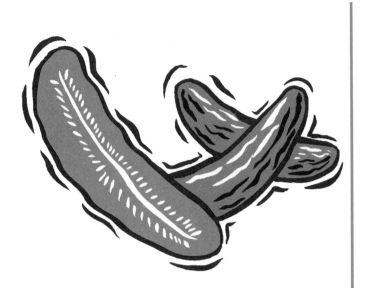

Knock, knock!
Who's there?
Kenny!
Kenny who?
Kenny let me in or what?

Knock, knock!
Who's there?
Ivana!
Ivana who?
Ivana suck your blood!

Knock, knock!
Who's there?
Pickle!
Pickle who?
Pickle lily and give it to your mother!

Knock, knock!
Who's there?
Gerald!
Gerald who?
Gerald if you can't hear me from this close!

Knock, knock!
Who's there?
Claire!
Claire who?
Claire the way! I'm coming through!

SILLY JOKES

What did the pastry say to the fresh bread?

"You've got a lot of crust!"

What was the elephant doing on the highway?

About 2 1/2 miles per hour!

Why can't two elephants go into the swimming pool at the same time?

Because they have only one pair of trunks!

What is long, orange, and shoots rabbits?

A double-barreled carrot!

What do you call an Italian lost in a Scottish mist?

A Roman in the gloamin'!

Why don't elephants ride bicycles?

Because they have no thumbs to work the bells!

What U.S. president lived near the sea and ate people?

Jaws Washington!

What would you call a giant legal shark?

The chief jawstice!

What has pretty wings, sits on flowers, and is deadly?

A man-eating butterfly!

What does the queen do when she burps?

Issues a royal pardon!

What is round, purple, and used to rule the world?

Alexander the Grape!

What leaves footprints all over the ocean floor?

A lemon sole!

What floats, weighs 250,000 tons, and tastes of tomato soup?

A soupertanker!

Where do you find baby soldiers?

In the infantry!

How does a fox feel after it has eaten a goose?

Down in the mouth!

Why does lightning shock people?

Because it doesn't know how to conduct itself!

What do fairies love to drink?

Sprite!

☆ ☀ ☆

What does a wizard call a naughty child?

A brat-cadabra!

☆ ☾ ☆

Where do wizards go for cold medicine?

To witch doctors!

☆ ☀ ☆

What is a gnome's favorite singer?

Elf-is Presley!

What did the wizard call the gnome who thought only of himself?

S-elf ish!

☆ ☾ ☆

When the student turned a dog into a cat, what did the wizard say?

"Con-cat-ulations! Hexellent job!"

☆ ☀ ☆

What sound do witches make when they start their transportation?

Brrrrroooooom, brrrrroooooom, brrrooooom!

☆ ☾ ☆

Knock, knock!
Who's there?
Ghost!
Ghost who?
Ghost to show, nobody remembers my name!

☆ ☀ ☆

What did the wizard say when he met the ghost?

"Well, good evening, sir. How do you boo?"

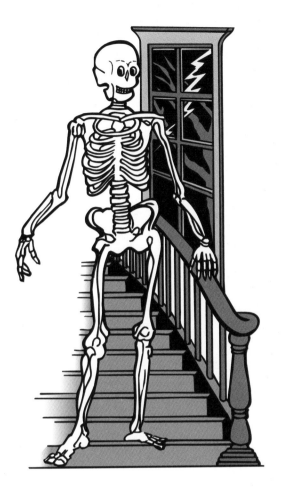

Why did the wizard turn himself into a skeleton?

Because his wife was getting under his skin!

What did she call him when she saw what he had done?

Gutless!

What did the wizard think of having vampire bats hanging from his roof?

He thought it was fang-tastic!

Why do dragons sleep all day?

So they can get out at knights!

What kind of teams did the monsters want when playing baseball?

Ghouls versus boys!

Why did the wizard think the vampire had a cold?

Because of all the coffin!

What did the surfer think after the wizard changed him into a frog?

He thought it was toad-ally awesome!

What did student say when told that he forgot everything he learned?

"Can you repeat the question?"

If the questions were so easy, why did the student fail?

It was the answers that were hard!

What did the student write about Noah?

That he was an ark-itecht!

When does history repeat itself?

When you fail it the first time around!

What did the student think about the condition of his chair?

Desk-picable!

What is the best class in school?

Recess!

Why couldn't Jimmy remember what he had read out loud?

He wasn't listening!

Why was the student late for school?

She was obeying the SLOW CHILDREN CROSSING sign!

Why did the student feel as if his pencil slowed him down?

Because it was made of lead!

How did the student scrape his knee?

On a class trip!

How did the student answer this exam question: "What happens to gold when exposed to air?"

"It gets stolen!"

What do students read in classrooms in the Lone Star State?

Tex-books!

Why do fish do so poorly in schools?

Because they're below "C" level!

Why did the student take a top hat and cape to her exam?

She was hoping to use math-magic! (mathematics)

What did the boxer shorts say to the airplane pilot's trousers?

"You're flying awfully low, aren't you?"

What kind of shorts do big cats wear?

Panther pants!

What do you call an underwear history book?

A brief history of time!

What do the writing instructions on a package of jockey shorts say?

"Keep in pouch!"

What did the man say when asked if his shorts had ripped right down the middle?

"Seams that way, doesn't it?"

What do boxer shorts think of this book?

It's unbe-brief-able!

How did the boxers feel after the man gained weight?

Stretched to the limit!

What did the old man think of breathable shorts?

He really cott-on to the idea!

What do you call shorts that have lost their elastic?

Ex-spandex!

What do you get when you put old underpants on an antenna?

A smelly telly!

Knock, knock!
Who's there?
Enid!
Enid who?
Enid a clean pair of underwear!

How do you tell someone that he needs new underwear?

Briefly!

What is it called when you take off your shorts at night?

De-briefing!

Why did the boxer shorts feel betrayed?

They felt that they had been hung out to dry!

Why should you always wear underwear to bed?

In case you get woken up on short notice!

What do felines wear to bed?

The cat's pajamas!

SILLY SPIES

What did the secret agent say when she heard about the giant spy?

"This sounds like a tall tale to me!"

How can you check to see if your friends are enemy agents?

With a spy-detector test!

Where did the secret agent find the sketch artist?

In the drawing room, of course!

Why don't piano spies ever catch an enemy?

Because they just can't get organized!

What did the secret agent say when he caught his enemy hiding under his bed?

"You're under a-rest!"

What did the secret agent say when he found his enemy hiding in his closet?

"You're under a-vest!"

What did the French spy say after hiding out in the rain all night?

"Eiffel a cold coming on!"

Why did the hacker give his computer a box of tissues?

Because it had a nasty virus!

What did the secret agent say when he finally captured his enemy, the Condor?

"Now you're a jailbird!"

What did the spy say when he was told to make a peephole in the wall?

"Yeah, I know the drill!"

Why did the peace-loving spy hate fiddles?

Because he didn't believe in violins! (violence)

What did the secret agent think about chasing her nemesis through the train?

That he was hard to keep track of!

What did the rock-climbing spy wear for jewelry?

Mountain-earrings!

What did the spy student think when he broke his pencil?

He thought it was pointless!

What do bikers call their annual scrapbooks?

The gearbook!

What did the biker do when he realized that he had insulted someone?

He really had to back-pedal!

How did the windsurfer get his gear so cheap?

It was on sail!

What did the diver have to say after the wedding ceremony?

"There wasn't a dry suit in the house!"

What is a windsurfer's favorite candy?

Life Savers, of course!

What did the one skater say about his friend's great Ollie story?

"Sounds like a tall tail to me!"

What do skaters call it when they skate to school with their lunches?

Meals on wheels!

Why are skaters so curious?

They stick their noses in everything!

What did the windsurfer think of the flashy new guy who couldn't turn?

She thought he lacked tack!

What did the kayaker say when the beginner said that he could beat him?

"Paddle be the day!"

What did the announcer say when she saw the two kayakers in a close finish?

"I don't know if it's one oar the other!"

What is the worst part about boarding before the season starts?

The climb to the top!

What do boarders and cowboys have in common?

Rodeo flips!

When is a snowboard like an old piano?

When it needs to be tuned!

What are the only commitments most boarders believe in?

Bindings!

How did the boarder get rid of her dullness?

She sharpened her board!

KNOCK, KNOCK!

Knock, knock!
Who's there?
Annie!
Annie who?
Annie body home?

Knock, knock!
Who's there?
Christine!
Christine who?
Christine that you don't live here anymore, but I told him you did!

Knock, knock!
Who's there?
Falafel!
Falafel who?
Falafel my skateboard and landed on my knee!

Knock, knock!
Who's there?
Island!
Island who?
Island on my feet when I jump!

Knock, knock!
Who's there?
Luck!
Luck who?
Luck through the keyhole!

Knock, knock!
Who's there?
Cook!
Cook who?
You're the one who's cuckoo!

Knock, knock!
Who's there?
Althea!
Althea who?
Althea later, alligathor!

Knock, knock!
Who's there?
Tarzan!
Tarzan who?
Tarzan stripes forever!

Knock, knock!
Who's there?
Scotland!
Scotland who?
*Scotland on his head.
We're gonna have to take him
to the hospital!*

Knock, knock!
Who's there!
Irish!
Irish who?
*Irish you'd take me
to the soccer game!*

Knock, knock!
Who's there?
Wales!
Wales who?
*Wales long as I'm here,
why don't we go out?*

Knock, knock!
Who's there?
Giovanni!
Giovanni who?
*Giovanni go to the park
with me?*

SILLY SPIES

What did the spy say when he couldn't find clues in the forest?

"I'm stumped!"

What did the enemy spy say when he couldn't find clues in the aluminum factory?

"Curses, foiled again!"

What happened to the agent-in-training who flunked spelling?

He was ex-spelled!

Secret agent: "What is your job like?

Sketch artist: "It has some draw-backs!"

What did the computer spy say when she found the enemy's plans?

"This is disk-usting!"

What did the spy say when he tied up his enemy in record time?

"Knot so fast!"

Why didn't the spy want to kiss the frog?

Because she was afraid it would croak!

How did the spy feel after spending a month in Turkey?

Stuffed!

What did the sleuth say after he had been out looking for clues all night?

"Owl never do that again!"

How long did the spy stay undercover in the tree house?

About a fort-night!

How do spies feel after lying low all the time?

A little flat!

What do secret agents use to look for their enemies?

Spy-noculars!

What did the spy say when he heard that there was an invisibility pill?

"I find that hard to swallow!"

What did the spy say when she got a splinter in her hand?

"Wooden you know it!"

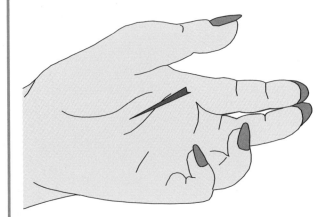

135

Wacky Wizardry

Wizard: Why don't you go to the pep rally?
Ghost: Why?
Wizard: To give them some school spirit!

How did the eight-legged creature know that he had met his true love?

He just spider!

What did the wizard say to the vain troll?

Oh, get ogre yourself!

What did the three ogres who lived under the wizard's bridge want to install?

A troll booth!

What do San Francisco ogres like better than the bus?

The troll-ey car!

What do you call bird ghosts?

Sea-ghouls!

What did the sick ghost say to the wizard when it got out of the hospital?

Do you want to hear about my apparition?

What did the wizard say to the vampire while it was still in its coffin?

Now listen, I don't want you to flip your lid!

Knock, knock!
Who's there?
Bats!
Bats who?
Bats a matter, don't you recognize me?

Why did the wizard call the ghost a phony?

Because he could see right through him!

What did the wizard use to open the tomb?

A skeleton key!

Dad wizard: Why do you want a lizard?

Kid wizard: "Because I-guana!"

What did the wizard call the foreign ghost?

An imported spirit!

When the ghost moved, what did it tell the wizard it would miss?

All of its possessions!

What did the wizard sing to the cowboy elf?

"Gnome on the Range"!

Why was the skeleton lonely?

Because he had no body to see!

Why couldn't the witch fly?

She was broom-sick!

XTREME-LY FUNNY

What did the extreme skier get his fiancée for their engagement?

A black diamond!

How did the skier decide to hide her skiing buddy's gear?

She took a pole!

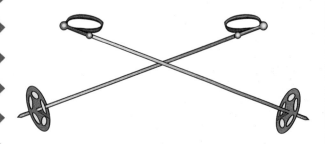

Why are big-hill skiers weird about relationships?

Because they're happy when they're on the Rockies!

What did the skier say after she added up the expenses for her trip?

"I guess that would summit up!"

What happened to the boarder who crashed on the pipe floor?

He was flat-bottom broke!

What do gliders and boarders have in common?

They both love hang time!

Why did the skater pretend that he was someone else?

Because he was riding fakie!

Why do boarders like to lie on their backs and watch the clouds?

Because they love the big air!

What did people say about the boarder who faceplanted?

I guess she needed to powder her nose!

What was the rider doing in the trees?

He had some trouble staying on track!

How did the ski racer sleep at night?

He needed to be all tucked in!

What do big-hill jumpers like most about their jobs?

The high life!

How did the boarder feel when he saw how much his new wraparounds cost?

He was goggle boggled!

What do boarders call lunch on the hill?

Frost bite!

What is it called when two bikers ride together?

a double cross!

What did the tired motocross biker need in the morning?

a kick-start!

KNOCK, KNOCK!

Knock, knock!
Who's there?
Justin!
Justin who?
Justin time for dinner!

Knock, knock!
Who's there?
Hey, Alex!
Hey Alex who?
*Hey, Alex the questions
around here!*

Knock, knock!
Who's there?
Larry!
Larry who?
*Larry funny, now open
the door!*

Knock, knock!
Who's there?
Otto!
Otto who?
*Otto be a law against
knock-knock jokes like these!*

Knock, knock!
Who's there?
Treachers!
Treachers who?
Treachers for you if you can guess!

Knock, knock!
Who's there?
Amy!
Amy who?
*Amy day now you could let
me inside!*

Knock, knock!
Who's there?
Homie!
Homie who?
Homie where the heart is!

Knock, knock!
Who's there?
Wendy!
Wendy who?
Wendy clock strikes twelve, it's lunch time!

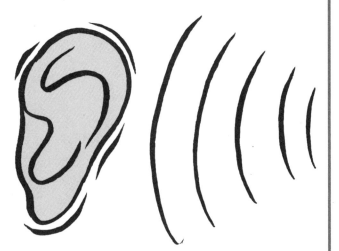

Knock, knock!
Who's there?
Daniella!
Daniella who?
Daniella so loud! I can hear you just fine.

Knock, knock!
Who's there?
Vanessa!
Vanessa who?
Vanessa good time to come back?

Knock, knock!
Who's there?
Holden!
Holden who?
Holden, I'll go see!

Knock, knock!
Who's there?
Marcus!
Marcus who?
Marcus down for two tickets. We're going to the show!

SILLY SPIES

What do you call a spy who specializes in spying on houses?

A real-estate agent!

What do you call someone who spies overseas?

A travel agent!

What do you call twin spies?

Double agents!

What do you call a villain who tells on other villains?

Gold Finker!

What was the code name of the spy sent to the North Pole?

Cold Finger!

How do spies make themselves look twice as good?

With bi-noculars!

How do decoding agents like their eggs?

Un-scrambled!

What did the spy use when he didn't know the answer on a test?

Guess-pionage!

Where do spies go when they die?

Underground!

Why did the retired spy think that he could be a blacksmith?

Because he knew how to forge things!

Why did the spy hide in the bushes?

Because she wanted to hedge her bets!

What do you call the secret records of forestry spies?

The Ax Files!

What did the secret agent use to break out of her cell?

An X-file!

What do you call a secret agent who just came back from Fort Knox?

The spy who came in from the gold!

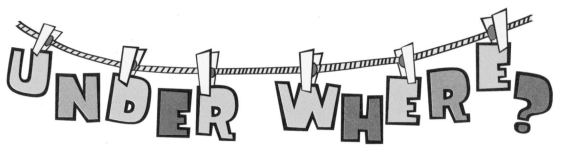

UNDER WHERE?

What did the canine say when her underwear ripped?

Doggone boxers!

What do wolves think of boxer-shorts jokes?

They think they're a howl!

What do owls think of boxer-shorts jokes?

They think they're a hoot!

What do you call it when boxer shorts get caught on a nail?

Under tear!

Knock, knock!
Who's there?
Sabrina!
Sabrina who?
Sabrina long time since I've changed my underwear!

Was the man nervous about how comfortable his new boxer shorts would be?

Yes, he was a little weary! (wary)

What do you call tiny boxer shorts for teddy bears?

Bear-ly theres!

What do you call a shop that sells boxer shorts in the forest?

Bear-ly wares!

Why did the sailor want his underwear to ride low?

So that people could see his naval!

What do you call the mama, papa, and baby underwear that live in the woods?

The three wears!

What do you say to people who won't stop telling underwear jokes?

You tell them to make it short!

What do you call someone who wears frilly shorts?

Mr. Fancy Pants!

What do you call underwear made of wood?

Birch boxers!

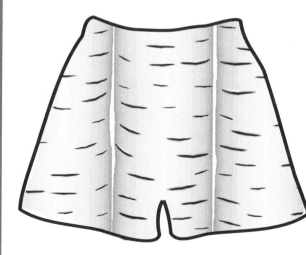

What do apes who make boxer shorts call their shop?

Monkey business!

What do artists wear on really hot days?

Just boxers and smocksers!

What do you call shorts with a back pocket?

A fanny pack!

Wacky Wizardry

Why did the wizard shrink his wife down to a tiny size?

Because he wanted a wrist-witch!

What did the witch's cat say about hunting giant rodents?

"I'd rat-her not!"

Why did the witch think her broom was so fast?

It had 300-hearse power!

What did she do about it?

She took the broom temperature!

Why do witches like shopping so much?

Because they love to hag-gle!

What did the wizard call his candle-making wife?

The wick-ed witch!

What did the wizard call the birds that haunted his backyard?

Polter-geese!

What did the wizard tell the student to do after dinner?

His gnomework!

Who helps the witch doctor?

The curse nurse!

☆ ☽ ☆

When the student got a wand, what did the wizard say?

"Why don't you try it out for a spell?"

☆ ☀ ☆

What did the wizard need after he spilled food on his outfit?

Soap on a robe!

What did he sing while he washed his outfit?

Robe-a-dub-dub!

☆ ☽ ☆

What happened when the student wizard was caught cheating?

He was ex-spelled!

What was the wizards' meeting group called?

Conjured citizens!

What did the wizard say to his daughter before the big test?

"Good luck on the hex-am!"

What do wizards give their spiders to eat?

Corn on the cobweb!

Pet Punchlines

What do you say to a sad-looking horse?

"Hey, why the long face?"

When should you tell your chickens to lay eggs?

On Fry-day!

What do you get when you take away one of your bunnies?

A hare less!

What do you use to write to your pet hog?

A pigpen!

Why should you never tell secrets to pet pigs?

Because they are bound to squeal!

Why didn't your uncle like your pet?

Because it's an aunt-eater!

What do you get if you have pygmy cows for pets?

Condensed milk!

What did the baby lizard say when it hatched in a terrarium?

"Hey, this isn't all it's cracked up to be!"

What do cats give each other on Valentine's Day?

Chocolate mousse!

What do pet mice keep locked in their trunks?

Chest nuts!

What do you say to a blue chameleon?

"Lighten up!"

How can a pet salamander spend all day in the rain and not get a single hair wet?

That's easy—salamanders don't have hair!

What do you call a pet monkey that is crazy for chocolate?

A cocoa nut!

How do you get your pet monkey to take you to school?

Drive it bananas!

 SILLY SPIES

Why did the spy think that he could dance?

Because he knew how to wire tap!

Where does a spy keep her leftovers?

Under wraps!

What does a spy wear under his pants?

Stealth bloomers!

What do secret agents drink their juice out of?

Spyglasses, of course!

How does a spy finish his book in the dark?

With infra-read glasses!

Why didn't the spy take any pictures while on vacation?

Because he had a hidden camera!

What did the secret agent call her stolen torch?

A flash-loot!

Where do secret agents live?

If I told you, it wouldn't be a secret anymore!

What do spies say to each other when they make a toast?

"Here's to your stealth!"

How do secret agents look for fingerprints?

With magni-spying glasses!

What do spies call a bad day of fishing?

Fishin' Impossible!

What do colorful secret agents wear?

Spy-dye!

What do spies call it when they take off their underwear?

De-briefing!

What do spies do when they have a slow day?

Mission wishin'!

XTREME-LY FUNNY

Where do most racers lose their concentration?

In the whoops!

What do most racers love to listen to on their stereos?

Their own track records!

What did the racer call the pig that tried the course?

A road hog!

What does a motocross racer do on the track?

About 60 mph!

What color was the catfish that the diver saw?

Purrrrple!

Why did the BMXer get into his dryer?

He just wanted to go for a spin!

Why did the racer show up in a suit of armor?

Because he heard that it was a knight race!

Why did the skier cry after he hit the tree?

It was a weeping willow!

How was the racer's experience crashing through the window?

Very pane-ful!

How did the in-line skaters afford their own bowl?

They just pooled their money!

Why was the bike racer doing laps around her bed?

She was trying to catch up!

What did the owl think of the boarders on the pipe?

It thought they were a hoot!

Where did the skater go after the back of her board broke off?

To the re-tail shop, of course!

Why couldn't the surfer sleep after having a close encounter with a shark?

He kept having bitemares!

Why did the boarders get caught by the sudden falling snow?

Because they stopped to ava-lunch!

KNOCK, KNOCK!

Knock, knock!
Who's there?
Yuni!
Yuni who?
Yuni to keep reading these knock-knock jokes!

Knock, knock!
Who's there?
Benny!
Benny who?
Benny-where interesting lately?

Knock, knock!
Who's there?
Tailor!
Tailor who?
Tailor head, your choice!

Knock, knock!
Who's there?
Tina!
Tina who?
Tina little bug just bit me right on the nose!

Knock, knock!
Who's there?
Freddie!
Freddie who?
Freddie or not, here I come!

Knock, knock!
Who's there?
Jess!
Jess who?
Hey, that's my line!

Knock, knock!
Who's there?
Who?
Who who?
I didn't know you were an owl!

Knock, knock!
Who's there?
Joanna!
Joanna who?
Joanna big kiss or what?

Knock, knock!
Who's there?
Anne Maureen!
Anne Maureen who?
Anne Maureen the lawn,
I'll talk to you later!

Knock, knock!
Who's there?
Jimmy!
Jimmy who?
Jimmy back my book, you thief!

Knock, knock!
Who's there?
Roger!
Roger who?
Roger be talking to someone
who knew me!

Knock, knock!
Who's there?
Coco!
Coco who?
Coco nuts are for monkeys,
not people!

Wacky Wizardry

How did the wizard's horse
do at the races?

She came in cursed place!

What did the wizard come up with
in the lab?

A brand-new hex-periment!

How did the wizard
get rid of termites?

He had them hex-terminated!

How did the wizard's wife feel
after she got fleas?

W-itchy!

What was the wizard's daughter
named in the beauty pageant?

Miss Tic! (mystic)

What do you call a dancing spirit?

The boogie man!

How did the wizard feel after he
heard the creepy music?

Ear-ee!

What did the tree say after the
ghost went through its leaves?

"Well, shiver me timbers!"

**What does a
ghost knight ride?**

A haunted horse!

☆ 🌙 ☆

**What do you call a tent
for the undead?**

A cree-pee!

☆ ☀ ☆

**How did the wizard get to his house
when the drawbridge was broken?**

With a rowmoat!

☆ 🌙 ☆

**How do wizards
get their soup?**

In can-tations!

**What do ghosts see
in a rainbow?**

A whole specter of colors!

**What did the wizard ask
his art class to do?**

Draw-bridge!

☆ ☀ ☆

**What did the wizard get while
he was rowing in his moat?**

Moat-shun sickness!

☆ 🌙 ☆

**How did the wizard find the
ingredients he needed for his spell?**

With a toad map!

157

TEACHER TICKLERS

What did the teacher say to the student who was late to school because he had overslept?

"You sleep at home, too?"

Teacher: "So you missed school yesterday?"

Student: "No, not even a bit!"

Teacher: "Are you passing notes at the back of the class?"

Student: "No, we're playing cards!"

Student: "I don't deserve a zero on this test!"

Teacher: "I agree, but there's nothing less I can give you!"

How did the student know that his teacher liked him?

When she asked him to come back next year and do it all over again!

What kind of teachers wear sunglasses?

Ones with bright students!

Why did the teacher close his eyes when he was in front of mirrors?

So he wouldn't have to see his pupils!

Why didn't the student answer the teacher?

Because he was taught not to talk back!

Teacher: "Why are you running into the classroom?"

Student: "You told me not to walk in late!"

What did the teacher say to the student who kept talking in class?

"Now you'll pay detention!" (attention)

Why did the teacher sit at a round desk?

So the students couldn't get him cornered!

What do teachers give on Halloween?

Blood tests!

Teacher: "You can't keep anything in your head for five minutes!"

Student: "Well, I've had this cold all day, haven't I?"

How did the teacher describe his class?

"They test my patience, so I test them right back!"

Teacher: "I hope I didn't just see you cheating!"

Student: "Me, too!"

SILLY SPIES

How do spy magicians
start their tricks?

By saying, "Pick a lock, any lock!"

How do computer spies know that
it's time to go to work?

They have a big hack attack!

What did the computer spy
take with him while
on assignment out of the office?

His field-mouse!

What do you call
a dim-witted spy?

Counter-intelligent!

What do you call a spy who is
always out of breath?

The Pink Pant-er!

What did the spy say
when she was questioned?

"I swear it's the sleuth!"

What do spy kids do for fun?

They go to Scout meetings!

Why did the spy keep checking
his timepiece?

Because he was told to
keep watch for the enemy!

How did the American spy find his foreign friend?

He did a background Czech!

What do you call a rural spy who talks?

An in-farmer!

What did the secret agent have for lunch?

A spy sub!

What do you call a ghost spy?

A spook!

What did the spy call the difficult task he was given?

Mission Improbable!

Why was the bounty hunter looking for a man with a tag in his hair?

Because she had heard that there was a price on his head!

SILLY JOKES

What do gorillas sing on Christmas?

**"Jungle Bells!
Jungle Bells!"**

What is a fjord?

A Norwegian motor car!

Why is it dangerous to play cards
in the jungle?

*Because of all
the cheetahs!*

What begins with *P*, ends in *E*, and
has a thousand letters?

Post office!

What happens when you cross a dog
with a giraffe?

*You get a pet that barks
at airplanes!*

What do cats read every morning?

Mewspapers!

Why do tennis players
have such a good life?

They have a real racket!

Who has eight guns
and terrorizes the ocean?

Billy the squid!

What do reindeer say before they
tell a joke?

"This one will sleigh you!"

What is Italian, 182 feet high, and delicious?

The Leaning Tower of Pizza!

What lies at the bottom of the sea and shivers?

A nervous wreck!

Why do soldiers like autumn?

Because of all the leaves!

What did Vikings use for secret messages?

Norse code!

How many bricks go into a house?

None. They all have to be carried!

How do scientists calculate the weight of whales?

They take them to a whale-weigh station!

Who is Santa Claus's wife?

Mary Christmas!

Where did the haunted suit of armor go for classes?

Knight school!

★ ☽ ★

What did the wizard call the knight who loved to joust?

Lance-a-lot!

★ ☀ ★

Why couldn't the knight go riding?

Because he had a horse throat!

★ ☽ ★

When the wizard tried to go riding, what did the horse say?

"Hoof got to be kidding!"

★ ☀ ★

What did the wizard say to stop the knight from fighting?

"Joust a moment!"

★ ☽ ★

What did the knight give his horse after a wedding?

A bridle sweet!

What did the knight do as he rode his horse along a riverbank?

He went trot fishing!

★ ☀ ★

What did the wizard make the knight do?

He made him sword on his life to stop fighting!

What did the wizard say about
the word *knight*?

It had a duel meaning!

⭐🌙⭐

What do you call the wizard's
unhappy feeling after riding the horse?

Sad-dle!

⭐☀️⭐

Why did the wizard get wet
when he was riding?

Because it was reining!

⭐🌙⭐

Knock, knock!
Who's there?
Boo!
Boo who?
*Hey, don't cry, I'm a
friendly ghost!*

What was the favorite fruit
of the wizard's horse?

Canter-lope!

⭐🌙⭐

What did the wizard's wife say when she
wanted to be covered in gold?

Alchem-me! (alchemy)

⭐☀️⭐

What did the wizard call the knight
who made lunch as he was riding?

The galloping gourmet!

What did the boarder say when her friend told her that her nose was running?

"No, it snot!"

Where do boarders keep their winnings?

In the snowbank!

What did the boarders think after they ran into one another?

They thought it was smashing!

How did the diver know that he had come upon some smart fish?

Because they were all still in school!

What did the doctor say about the skier who accidentally swallowed a quarter?

No change yet!

Bike-store owner: "These new bikes are $300 apiece."

Biker: "But I want the whole thing!"

How did the jellyfish surprise the surfer?

It stung into action!

What did the skater say when he saw sparks coming off the back of his board?

"Someone must be hot on my tail!"

What did the chairlift operator think about the skiers?

She thought they were a drag!

Why did the diver never trust the jellyfish?

Because he could see right through it!

What do you call a dangerous deep-sea dive?

An emergen-sea!

Why was the surfer worried about getting water in his ears?

He thought he might get brainwashed!

What did the old boarder call his ancient injuries?

His dino-sores!

Why was the boarder so good with her nose tricks?

She knew how to picket!

How did the boarder behave toward his buddy who pushed him into the snow?

He gave him the cold shoulder!

What is a good lunch for skiers?

Ice-bergers!

KNOCK, KNOCK!

Knock, knock!
Who's there?
Jo!
Jo who?
Jo, team, Jo!

Knock, knock!
Who's there?
Juana!
Juana who?
*Juana hear some more
knock-knock jokes?*

Knock, knock!
Who's there?
Harold!
Harold who?
Harold are you, anyway?

Knock, knock!
Who's there?
Cathy!
Cathy who?
*Cathy crook before he
geths away!*

Knock, knock!
Who's there?
Copperfield!
Copperfield who?
Copperfield sick,
so I came instead!

Knock, knock!
Who's there?
Frank Lee!
Frank Lee who?
Frank Lee my dear, I don't
give a darn!

Knock, knock!
Who's there?
Joey!
Joey who?
*Joey to the world!
It's Christmas!*

JOEY TO THE WORLD

Knock, knock!
Who's there?
Rain!
Rain who?
Rain deer! You remember me, the
one with the shiny red nose?

Knock, knock!
Who's there?
Snow!
Snow who?
Snow way I'm going out there.
It's freezing!

Knock, knock!
Who's there?
Suzy!
Suzy who?
Suzy opens the door, grab him!

Knock, knock!
Who's there?
Everest!
Everest who?
Everest your eyes during
the middle of class?
The teacher hates that!

Knock, knock!
Who's there?
Eddy!
Eddy who?
Eddy idea how I can get
rid ub dis cold?

SILLY SPIES

How did the spy feel when she tripped a wire at the embassy?

Alarmed!

Where do spies plant their secret gardens?

Behind investi-gates!

What did they say about the successful spy?

He had a great track record!

What do you call a snoop with sticky feet?

A gumshoe!

What do you call a sleuth with a big bill?

Private Duck!

What did the spy call the secret hideout in the woods?

A real mis-tree!

What do you call a detective with an eye patch?

A pirate investigator! Arrr!

Why do farmers make good secret agents?

Because they don't mind raking a little muck!

Why did the spy hate potatoes?

Because all the eyes made him nervous!

Why did the spy have to be quiet in the cornfield?

Because ears were everywhere!

Why do ghosts make good detectives?

Because they're not afraid to find skeletons in the closet!

What did the spy say when he was caught by the government?

"Gee, man!" (G-man)

What did the spy say after she processed her film?

"This is an interesting development!"

What do you call a great spy?

A super snooper!

Wacky Wizardry

What did the wizard call the princess who woke up angry from her long slumber?

Slapping beauty!

☆ ☽ ☆

What did the wizard give his wife when he wanted to protect her?

A suit of arm-her!

☆ ☀ ☆

Who was the favorite knight of the wizard's horse?

Donkey-oatey! (Don Quixote)

☆ ☽ ☆

How did the wizard clean his dog?

He made sham-poodle!

What did the wizard say to his dog after cleaning him?

My, don't you look houndsome!

☆ ☽ ☆

What did the wizard want for a scary dog?

A terror-er (terrier)!

☆ ☀ ☆

What did the wizard's dog do after a long run?

It lay down in a poodle of sweat!

☆ ☽ ☆

What was the wizard's dog's favorite vegetable?

Collie-flower!

Witch #1: "Are you sure that you don't want another cat?

Witch #2: "I'm paw-sitive!"

What kind of dog do zombies own?

Rot-weilers!

What did the wizard call his dog when it was unhappy?

Melon-collie!

What did the wizard give his cat for Easter?

Chocolate-covered mouse!

What did the wizard's cat say to the mirror?

"Don't you look purr-fect?"

What did the wizard's daughter say after he told her that he had changed her into a cat?

"Well, that's mews to me!"

How did the wizard give the cat what it wanted?

Easy. He made copy-cats!

What did the wizard's cat say when it hurt its paw?

"Me-ow!"

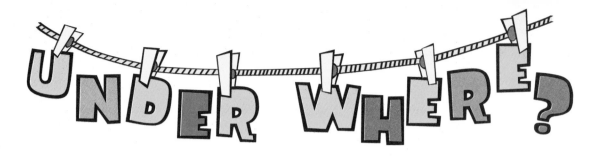

UNDER WHERE?

What do you call unattractive underwear that are too small?

Ugly snugglies!

What do you call a place where boxer shorts roam free?

The fanny farm!

What kind of card game do boxer shorts like to play?

Britch! (bridge)

Knock, knock!
Who's there?
Ice cream!
Ice cream who?
Ice creamed when my underpants fell down!

What do you call someone who steals your long underwear?

A woolly bully!

When is it bad to let someone put long johns on your head?

When he's trying to pull the wool over your eyes!

What kind of underwear did the heavy-weight champion wear while training?

Shadow-boxers!

What did one silk spinner say to the other?

Don't try to worm your way out of this!

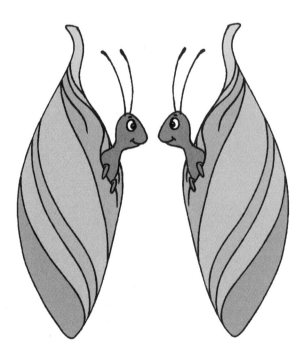

How did the farmer feel about taking away all the wool to make underwear?

A little sheepish!

How did the farmer feel about his healthy herd for the underwear season?

He thought they were in sheep shape!

What did the sheep call their cross-country journey?

A trip from shorn to shorn!

What did the sheep say when it narrowly avoided having its wool taken to market?

"That was a close shave!"

How did the farmer export her wares to the underwear shop?

She had them sheeped out!

How do sheep feel about woollen underwear?

Freezing!

How did the sheep feel about the crazy farmer who took all their wool for underwear?

They thought that it was shear madness!

What did the man think about his cherry-patterned underwear?

He thought they looked short but sweet!

CLASSROOM Crack-ups

What did the student think about his marks?

Lesson I thought!

Why did the student bring in the yield warning?

She thought that it would make a good a-sign-ment!

YIELD AHEAD

Why didn't the Alaskan student go to class?

He was too cool for school!

How did the student fail everything except math?

He didn't take math!

Why were the parents happy that their son was failing?

Because at least they knew he wasn't cheating!

Teacher: "You will have five minutes for each question."
Student: "How long do we get for the answers?"

What did the student say when told to draw a horse?

"Shouldn't the horse draw me?"

What did the student call the art contest?

Quick, draw!

What did the student think of the underwater science fair?

That it was a little fishy!

How do you know that you're at the top of your class?

When you're climbing rope in phys ed!

What do you call the bully in phys ed?

Gym Nastics!

Why didn't the student want to study English?

Because she wanted to study American!

Teacher: "This doctor's note is in your handwriting."

Student: "She borrowed my pen!"

What did the student say when the teacher told him to stop daydreaming?

"I wasn't! I was sound asleep!"

SILLY SPIES

What did the sick spy say about her code name?

"I don't like this ail-ias!"

What did one secret agent tell the other when he saw that it was raining?

"Make sure you put on your rain code!"

What did the spy say when she found out that the king's son was missing?

"We'll have to dust for prince!"

What do you call a spying royal with a shoe phone?

The foot prince!

How did the unhappy spy feel when he had no leads?

He had the no-clues blues!

Why was the left-handed spy so afraid of being arrested?

Because she didn't want to be read her rights!

What do you call a spy who is slow to look for clues?

A slowpoke!

What does a spy use to look for clues on a lawn?

Magnifying grass!

How do spies dress for fancy dinners?

In-former attire!

What do you call a story about a spy who spills the beans?

A tattletale!

What kind of bird always talks under pressure?

A stool pigeon!

What do you call a royal who has been arrested for spying?

A finger-prince!

Why is it hard to get a date when you're a spy?

Because everyone thinks you're creepy!

What advice do you give to a spy who can't open a window?

"If at first you don't succeed, pry, pry again!"

Wacky Wizardry

What did the wizard's daughter say when her cat was missing?

"This is a cat-astrophe!"

☆🌙☆

What did the wizard call the stone felines guarding the entrance to his castle?

Cat-er-pillars!

☆☀☆

What did the rodent say to the wizard?

"Mice to meet you!"

☆🌙☆

What did the witch call the gloves that she made for her cat?

Kitten mittens!

☆☀☆

Knock, knock!
Who's there?
Gnome!
Gnome who?
Gnome 'atter how many times I knock, you won't let me in!

Where did the wizard take his wife in the winter?

To the Snow Ball!

☆☀☆

Why were the fish in the moat so smart?

They were always in a school!

☆🌙☆

What did the wizard say when he saw the cat fly over the castle wall?

"Must be the cat-a-pult!"

What did the fish in the moat
play after school?

Trout or dare!

☆ 🌙 ☆

What did the witch say when she
fell into the moat?

My eels are killing me!

What did the wizard say when he heard
the mermaids singing?

"Those fish are out of tuna!"

☆ ☀ ☆

Where did the fish in the moat never
want to end up?

In squid row!

What is the wizard's favorite
fish lullaby?

"Salmon-chanted Evening"!

☆ ☀ ☆

How did the wizard know that he had
caught a big fish in his moat?

He could tell by the scales!

☆ 🌙 ☆

What did the fish say to its friend
when a horse fell into the moat?

"See horse?"

☆ ☀ ☆

KNOCK, KNOCK!

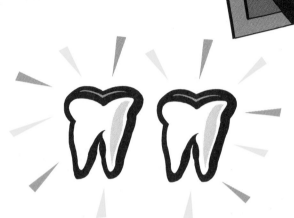

Knock, knock!
Who's there?
Penny!
Penny who?
Penny for your thoughts!

Knock, knock!
Who's there?
Agatha!
Agatha Who?
Agatha sore tooth! It's killing me!

Knock, knock!
Who's there?
Harry!
Harry who?
Harry up and take me
to the dentist!

Knock, knock!
Who's there?
Ollie!
Ollie who?
Ollie want for Christmas is
my two front teeth!

Knock, knock!
Who's there?
Becka!
Becka who?
Becka the bus is
the best place to sit!

Knock, knock!
Who's there?
Heidi Claire!
Heidi Claire who?
Heidi Claire, something
smells delicious!

Knock, knock!
Who's there?
Emma!
Emma who?
Emma too early for lunch?

Knock, knock!
Who's there?
Jimmy!
Jimmy who?
Jimmy a chance, and I know
I can make the team!

Knock, knock!
Who's there?
George!
George who?
George us day, isn't it!

Knock, knock!
Who's there?
Apple!
Apple who?
Apple your hair if you say no!

Knock, knock!
Who's there?
Juanita!
Juanita who?
Juanita sandwich with me?

Knock, knock!
Who's there?
Herman!
Herman who?
Herman grew a moustache
and his friends hate it!

XTREME-LY FUNNY

Why was the skater worried about his 11-inch nose?

He thought it might turn into a foot!

Two mountain bikers were lost in the damp clouds. One asked the other where they were. What did his friend say?

"I haven't the foggiest idea!"

What did friends call the racer who crumbled under pressure?

Crackers!

Why was the boarder crying?

Because he got hit in the eye with a snow bawl!

Why didn't the motocross racer get her dog a license?

Because she knew that they would never let it compete!

What did the boarder say when he saw the peg-legged pirate on the pipe?

"Wooden you know it!"

What did the dim-witted boarder say when his friend told him that he had put his boots on the wrong feet?

"But these are the only feet I have!"

What did the spectator at the downhill race say when asked about the scenery?

"I didn't see much. All these mountains were in front of it!"

Why did the lovesick skier wipe out so badly?

Because he was head over heels!

**Knock, knock!
Who's there?
Falafel!
Falafel who?
Falafel my skateboard and hurt my knee!**

Why did the competitive racer stay in bed with a fever of 103°?

He was going for the world record!

What breakfast cereal do skiers eat?

Flakes!

How did the girl and boy boarders know that they had fallen for each other on the mountaintop?

They knew it was love at first height!

Why was the skater worried about going crazy from having holes in her pockets?

She was afraid of losing her marbles!

Dad: "I got a snowboard for your little sister."

Boarder: "Really? That's an amazing deal!"

What did the boarder say when her friend commented that her socks didn't match?

"I have a pair at home just like these!"

SILLY SPIES

Why did the spy hate writing reports on his computer?

Because he just wasn't that type!

What did the skating spy say when he dropped his computer files on the ice?

"Oh, no! I've got a slipped disk!"

What made the robot secret agent act crazy?

He had a couple of screws loose!

How did the spy feel after hiding in a mine all day?

A little coaled!

What do you call it when a spy almost gets shot by a crossbow user?

An arrow escape!

What did the secret agent think about spying at the zoo?

That it was aardvark! (hard work)

Why was the female spy sent behind enemy lines?

Because it was a no-man's land!

What do spies wear when they are in the desert?

Camel-flage!

What did the sick spy think when his doctor told him that he was just ducky?

He thought the doctor was a quack!

What did the spy say about her job on the moon?

"It lacked atmosphere!"

What did the spy say when he had to row himself back to shore?

"This is oar-ibble!"

What did the secret agent say to the space-age spy?

"Pleased to meteor!"

Secret agent #1: "Hey, would you please call me a cab?"

Secret agent #2:"OK. You're a cab!"

What made the spy think that he had evidence against the lint?

Because he had it all on tape!

TEACHER TICKLERS

What did the student say when the teacher asked him to pay a little attention?

"I'm paying as little as I can!"

What does the teacher call doing your homework?

Detention prevention!

What did the student say when the teacher asked where her paper was?

"Es-say I forgot it!"

Why did the teacher want to teach at a school in the country after working in the city?

He had heard that the population was less dense in the country!

Teacher: "You haven't made anything all day!"

Student: "I've made a lot of mistakes. Don't they count?"

How did the teacher know that the student's father hadn't helped with her homework?

All the answers were wrong!

What did the student say when the teacher told him to answer at once?

"At once!"

At once!

**What do you call
a religion professor?**

A preacher teacher!

**What do you call
an economics teacher?**

A dollar scholar!

**Why did the math teacher wish
that her student was like a rabbit?**

*She wanted him to
multiply faster!*

**How did the spelling teacher
spell relief?**

S-U-M-M-E-R!

**What did the teacher call the
visit to a potato farm?**

A field trip!

Teacher: **"Even a six-year-old
could answer that question!"**

*Student: "No wonder I don't know
it! I'm too old!"*

**Why did the teacher have to tell his
student that she was failing math?**

*Because the student wasn't so
good with numbers!*

Wacky Wizardry

What did the wizard get when he crossed an owl with a goat?

A hoot 'n' nanny! (hootenanny)

What did the witch eat for breakfast?

Dreaded wheat!

What did the wizard get when he crossed a cow with a nap?

A bulldozer!

What did the wizard get when he crossed a toad with a lizard?

A croakadile!

Where do ghosts go swimming?

In the Dead Sea!

What kind of food do elves like to make?

Shortbread!

What did the wizard get when he crossed a cow with a washing machine?

A milk shake!

What did the wizard say about the stupid skeleton?

In one ear and out the other!

What did the wizard get when he crossed a whale with candy?

Blubber gum!

Pirate: How much will it cost to get my ears pierced?

Wizard: A buck an ear! (buccaneer)

⭐🌙⭐

How did the wizard's dog put the movie on hold?

He hit the paws button!

⭐☀️⭐

What did the wizard get when he crossed a lightbulb with his hometown?

Electri-city!

⭐🌙⭐

What kind of shoes do frogs wear?

Open-toad sandals!

Why couldn't the ghost see the wizard?

He wasn't wearing his spooktacles!

Why did the wizard need a monitor for his pet?

Because it was a computer mouse!

What did the ghost say to his wife?

"Hello, boo-tiful!"

Pet Punchlines

Where do dogs love to hang out?

In the barking lot!

How do watchdogs get wound up?

They run in circles!

What is your dog's favorite vegetable?

Pup-corn!

What kind of dog loves to be washed?

The shampoodle!

What kind of dog has a bark but never makes noise?

A dogwood tree!

What kind of pet can always tell you the time?

A watchdog!

What is the best kind of animal to take on long road trips?

A car pet!

Where is the one place a dog won't shop?

A flea market!

192

Why do cowboys love dachshunds for pets?

They like to get a long, little doggie!

What kind of dream woke up the horse?

A nightmare, of course!

What kind of soda does your pet frog like best?

Cherry croak!

What did the cat say when it cornered a mouse?

Mice to eat you!

What did Hansel and Gretel's cat like best about the forest?

The gingerbread mouse!

When should you take your pet chicks to the vet?

When it's time for their rooster shots!

KNOCK, KNOCK!

Knock, knock!
Who's there?
Homer!
Homer who!
Homer again after a long day of school. Time to have some fun!

Knock, knock!
Who's there?
Jason!
Jason who?
Jason your brother around the house will get you in trouble!

Knock, knock!
Who's there?
Wah Zeen!
Wah Zeen who?
Wah Zeen me who broke your window, honest!

Knock, knock!
Who's there?
Howell!
Howell who?
Howell I ever get in if you don't open the door?

Knock, knock!
Who's there?
Daisy!
Daisy who?
Daisy goes to school, nights he plays baseball!

Knock, knock!
Who's there?
Polly!
Polly who?
Polly wogs are just baby frogs!

Knock, knock!
Who's there?
Diane!
Diane who?
Diane to play football, let's go!

Knock, knock!
Who's there?
Jerry!
Jerry who?
Jerry funny. You know
who it is!

Knock, knock!
Who's there?
Peter!
Peter who?
Peter me! You're just going to have to
decide, once and for all, which of us
it's going to be!

Knock, knock!
Who's there?
Pucker!
Pucker who?
Pucker up, I'm gonna kiss you!

Knock, knock!
Who's there!
Dana!
Dana who?
Dana talk to me like that!

Knock, knock!
Who's there?
Alfred!
Alfred who?
Alfred I got the wrong door.
Sorry!

SILLY SPIES

What did they call the double agent who was always calling home?

A phone-y!

What do you call a spy who ends up in jail?

Con-fidential!

Why was the spy looking in the want ads?

Because the information she needed was classified!

What code name did they give to the spy who chewed gum?

Bubble-oh-seven!

What did the secret agent say when he had tracked down the lost goalie?

"Finders keepers!"

What did the secret agent say when she was looking for the missing livestock?

"Ollie, ollie, oxen free!"

What do spies put at the top of every memo?

Re: search!

What did the spy say when he left his papers in his filing cabinet?

"I'll have to check with the Bureau on that one!"

What did the computer spy get from the Internet virus?

A hacking cough!

What did the secret agent say when he mistook a bison for a cow?

"Sorry, it was an ox-idant!"

Where did the detective find the missing porridge?

In the mush-room!

What did the spy say when he woke to find two Xs written on him?

"I've been double-crossed!"

What do rude spies use to communicate?

Coarse code!

What do you call a spy with bad posture?

A stooped snoop!

197

Wacky Wizardry

What did the wizard say when he saw a bull in the sky?

"It must be a bull moon!"

☆ ☾ ☆

When did the dragon finally get full?

Around mid-knight!

☆ ☼ ☆

What do you call the wizard who is hungry for astronomy?

Star-ving!

☆ ☾ ☆

What did the witch say for a spell to get jewelry?

"Boil and bauble!"

Where did the wizard keep the power source for his basement?

In the dungeon-erator!

☆ ☾ ☆

What did the wizard call the statues on his walls when the sun made them hot?

Gar-boils!

☆ ☼ ☆

Where did the wizard keep the seeds for his garden?

Up in the flower tower!

What did the wizard get when he crossed a skunk with a TV set?

Smell-o-vision!

What did the wizard say about the stupid monarch?

"He ruled the whole king-dumb!"

What did the wizard call the young royal who kept falling down?

Prince Harming!

What did the wizard call the king who wouldn't come down out of the tower?

His Royal High-ness!

What did the wizard call the king of the monsters in Scotland?

His Loch Ness Highness!

What did the wizard say when he had to sell one of his paintings?

"It's only a poor-trait!"

How did the monster scare the wizard?

He crypt up on him!

Why did the wizard's butler wear a suit of armor?

Because he was a Sir-vant!

Where did the wizard go to withdraw a crystal ball?

To a fortune teller!

Why did the boy tell his father to go sit on the ski hill?

Because his mother wanted a cold pop!

What was the surfer named Ace most afraid of?

Card sharks!

What did the boarder say when he saw his sibling sticking partway out of the snow?

"Hey, look, it's my half-brother!"

What did the young surfer say about the old surfer who worked at the seafood restaurant?

"I can't believe she soled out!"

What did the skier say about the snowboarding feline?

"Now that's one cool cat!"

What do you call the part of a wooden surfboard without holes?

Knot holes!

Police officer: "I'll teach you to skate here, young man!"

Skater: "I wish you would. We keep wiping out!"

Knock, knock!
Who's there?
Island!
Island who?
Island perfectly every time I skydive!

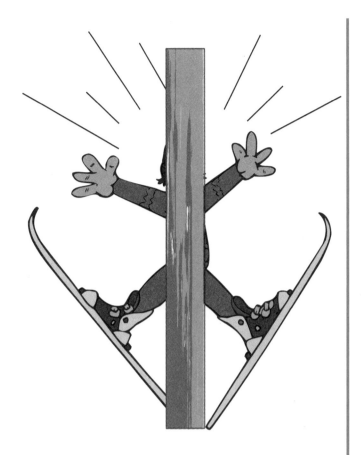

What did the skater say after skating behind a car for a few minutes?

"Man, I'm exhausted!"

What did the surfboard say to the termite?

"Stop boring me!"

Why did the diver fill his pockets with pencils?

He thought the lead would weigh him down!

Why did the surfer bail so big his first time on television?

Because he wanted to make a big splash!

How did the skier feel when he ran into the telephone pole?

He was shocked!

What did the shark say when it saw the surfers pull up in a Jeep?

"Look, canned food!"

What did the surfers say while they waited for the tide to come in?

"Long time, no sea!"

UNDER WHERE?

What do you call someone who wears camouflage boxers?

Under cover!

Knock, knock!
Who's there?
Izzy!
Izzy who?
Izzy wearing any underwear?

What do you call stockings that blow in the breeze?

Wind socks!

What did the designer think about her new line of hosiery?

She thought it was a big sock-sess!

What do you call a Scottish stocking puppet?

The Sock-Ness monster!

Why do you put wet shorts on the clothesline?

So they'll be high and dry!

Why did the boxer shorts like being on the clothesline?

They just started to get the hang of it!

Why didn't the boxer shorts want to be put away?

Because they thought it would hamper their style!

How did the dress feel about the see-through tights?

Sheer delight!

Why did the socks feel so confident?

Because they knew that they were a shoe-in!

What do you call all your favorite underwear when it's together for the first time?

A boxed set!

How quickly did the young man put on his boxers?

In a zip!

What kind of insect lives in some underwear?

The button fly!

What do you call the peg where you hang up your underwear?

The butt-on!

Knock, knock!
Who's there?
Butter!
Butter who?
Butter make sure your underwear isn't showing!

What is it called when someone works out in his underwear?

Boxer-cize!

SILLY SPIES

What do you call testimony that doesn't stand up in court?

Wilt-ness!

What do you ask a secret agent to do in court?

Testi-spy!

What do you pay a secret agent to speak in court?

Testi-money!

What did the secret agent call the bowling ball that she took to court?

Heavy-dence!

What did the spy say when he split his pants?

"Let me check my briefs!"

Where did the secret agent find the enemy chef?

In her hidden fork-tress!

How did the heavy spy escape?

He dug a ton-el!

What did the sign on the nuclear lab's door say when the spy arrived?

"Gone fission!"

Where did the spy have to go to find the enemy spy's baker?

To his secret breadquarters!

What did the spy wearing shorts say to the secret agent?

"Meet me at the cutoffs!"

Why did the spy know to look for the enemy agent in the wild?

Because he was a cheat-ah!
(cheetah)

How did the spy know that his enemy would come out of her underground lair?

Because she always caved in!

What did the spy say when she caught someone snooping in her front yard?

"Stop in the name of the lawn!"

What did the detective say when he caught the cold-hearted killer?

"Freeze!"

Wacky Wizardry

What did the wizard get when he crossed a python with a drinking cup?

A snake in the glass!

What did the wizard call the cow that went over the moon?

High jumper!

What did the wizard call the horse's back?

A mane frame!

What kind of nuts do frogs like?

Croak-o-nuts!

Where did the country wizard go to get supplies?

The farm-acy!

How did the wizard feel when a satellite fell into his yard?

Star struck!

When the young wizard turned a dog into a frog, what did his father say?

"What did I tell you about cursing in the house?"

WOOF!

How did the star-happy wizard like to eat his cookies?

With a Milky Way!

What did the astronomer wizard sing in the bath?

"When You Wash Upon a Star"!

What did the wizard get when he stuck his nose in a jar?

Ring around the nosie!

What dish do goblins like best?

Mon-stir fry!

Why do wizards have stars and moons on their hats?

They need a little personal space!

What do wizards put in potions to make people gain weight?

In-greed-ients!

What color was the wizard's cat?

Purr-ple!

What do you call a wizard who loves telescopes?

Astrono-merlin!

What did the wizard say about the rowboat going around the moat?

"Looks like it's in oar-bit!"

KNOCK, KNOCK!

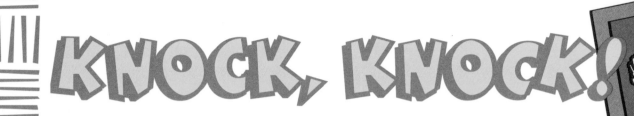

Knock, knock!
Who's there?
Sheepritty!
Sheepritty who?
Sheepritty, don't you think?

Knock, knock!
Who's there?
Deannie!
Deannie who?
Deannie hear me the first time?

Knock, knock!
Who's there!
Chuck!
Chuck who?
Chuck me the ball and quit asking so many questions!

Knock, knock!
Who's there?
Fishes!
Fishes who?
Fishes temper that dog's got. He should be on a leash!

Knock, knock!
Who's there?
Disguise!
Disguise who?
Disguise killing me with these knock-knock jokes!

Knock, knock!
Who's there?
Emma!
Emma who?
Emma bugging you yet?

Knock, knock!
Who's there?
Chair!
Chair who?
Chair you go again, asking
silly questions!

Knock, knock!
Who's there?
Amy!
Amy who?
Amy 'fraid I may have the
wrong house! You don't look
familiar at all!

Knock, knock!
Who's there?
Discus!
Discus who?
Discus throwing inside will
get you detention!

Knock, knock!
Who's there?
Holly!
Holly who?
Holly cow, Boss, it's time to head
back to the hideout!

Knock, knock!
Who's there?
Doughnut!
Doughnut who?
Doughnut make me reveal my true
identity! I'm undercover!

Knock, knock!
Who's there?
Patty O.!
Patty O. who?
Patty O'Furniture!

 ILLY SPIES

Why was the spy so afraid of insects?

Because he knew that he was being bugged!

What did the spy say when she found out that her phone was being tapped?

"When will these guys stop bugging me?"

What did the doctor write in the spy's fitness report?

"This agent is in tip-tap shape!"

What do you call a spy who's a bug?

Insect-or Gadget!

Why did the spy go to work dressed as a bee?

Because she'd heard there was going to be a sting!

What did the spy do when he heard that he had to dig a tunnel?

He tried to worm his way out of it!

What did the detective say to the chicken?

"I have to appre-hen-d you!"

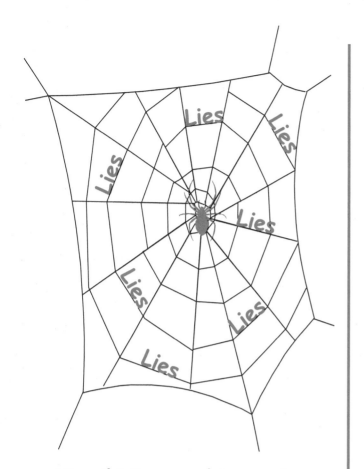

Why did the spy nickname her enemy "The Spider"?

Because he lived in a web of lies!

What did the spy say to the bee?

"Buzz off!"

What did the spy have to take after being bitten by a bug?

Ant-ibiotics!

Why did the detective think that the spy had wings?

Because he was a fly-by-night!

How did the spy get to the honey?

*She followed the bee-trail!
(betrayal)*

What do you call a wire-tapping rabbit spy?

Bugs bunny!

What kind of critters do secret agents like?

Spy-ders!

How does it feel to sit in front of a fire after skiing all day?

Grate!

Why did the motocrosser ride his bike?

Because it was too heavy to carry!

What was the highest mountain before Mt. Everest was discovered?

Mt. Everest!

Knock, knock!
Who's there?
Olaf!
Olaf who?
Olaf my skis at the bottom of the hill!

What did the young surfer say to the old surfer, who could remember when a phone call cost 10 cents?

"Hey, dimes have changed!"

Why don't boarders ever wear watches?

Because they know that time flies!

Why did the hang glider put his watch on the ground?

He wanted to fly over time!

Why did the climber take her watch up the mountain with her?

She wanted to see time travel!

Why did the skateboarder take a pumpkin off the jump with him?

Because he wanted to make squash!

What did the dirty biker say when it started to rain really hard?

"If this keeps up, my name will be mud!"

What did the tired mountain biker say after crashing into the shrubs?

"Man, am I bushed!"

Did you hear the story about the skateboarder who snapped the back of her board?

It's a sad tail!

Why did the surfer wipe out?

Because he was blinded by the sunfish!

Why was the surfer so happy to swim with dolphins?

Because she felt that she really had a porpoise!

What did the wizard call his favorite reptile?

The Lizard of Oz!

★ ☽ ★

What is the wizard's favorite swamp flower?

The croak-us!

★ ☀ ★

What did the frog say to his son who was late for school?

"Hop to it!"

Why did the wizard say that you should never warm up to a snake?

Because they're cold-blooded!

★ ☽ ★

What did the wizard call his hallways after he had snakeskin wallpaper installed?

His rept-aisles!

★ ☀ ★

What animal does the wizard say is always lying?

The bull-frog!

What did the wizard use to warn other drivers that he was coming?

A frog-horn!

☆ 🌙 ☆

What did the wizard's son say when the wizard started to tell him the reptile joke?

"You already toad me that one!"

☆ ☀ ☆

How do frogs get clean?

They use croak-on-a-rope!

☆ 🌙 ☆

What do you call the wizard who collects wildlife from the swamp?

A toad-hog!

Where did the wizard go to turn the student back into a boy?

The changing room!

☆ ☀ ☆

What did the wizard call his smallest fishing rod?

A tad-pole!

☆ 🌙 ☆

What did the cat in the wizard's castle have to do?

Mousework!

☆ ☀ ☆

What did the wizard say when his cat caught a mouse?

"Micely done!"

☆ 🌙 ☆

What did the wizard's blackbird think about the big party?

Oh, he was raven about it!

☆ ☀ ☆

Was the wizard's blackbird hungry after the party?

He was raven-ous!

COMIC CRITTERS

What is the coolest animal
in the swamp?

The hip-o!

What do you call a sleeping lizard?

A calm-eleon!

How do you know that you've
seen a leopard?

Oh, they're easy to spot!

What do you see when a bear has
its head in a blueberry bush?

Its bear bottom!

What are the first notes of
the monkeys' 5th Symphony?

Ba-na-na-na!

What kind of animal has the best
color in summer?

The orangu-tan!

What do you call a seat
for a frog?

A toad-stool!

Who can you use to make calls
in a swamp?

A croc-o-dial!

What birds are twice as fun
as the rest?

*The cock-a-two and the
pair-a-keet!*

Where do you put your
jumping friends from Australia?

In the kanga-room!

What animal is no fun at a party?

The boar!

SILLY SPIES

Why did the secret agent look for clues in a pasture?

Because he wanted to do his first field assignment!

What happened to the sketch artist?

He disappeared without a trace!

What did the detective say to the dessert?

"I have to put you in protective custard-y!"

What do secret agents do for fun?

Play catch!

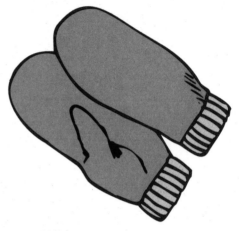

Why did Soviet spies always wear mittens?

Because they were in the Cold War!

What did the silly sleuth say to the conductor?

"I have to de-train you for questioning!"

Why do spies love the snow?

Because it's a hint-er wonderland!

Why was the spy worried about his socks while spying on the golfers?

Because he had a hole in one!

What did the sick secret agent say to the criminal?

"Hold out your hands so I can cough (cuff) you!"

What did the secret agent say to the Riddler?

"I have to take you in for questioning!"

Why did the spy follow her enemy to the races?

Because she wanted to track him down!

Why was the spy hiding in the butcher shop?

Because she thought that was where the steak-out was!

What do you call it when a secret agent comes out of hiding?

Dis-cover!

Why was the spy afraid of airplanes?

She was afraid that someone would identi-fly her!

XTREME-LY FUNNY

What did the boarder say when she slipped on a banana skin?

"I didn't find that very a-peeling!"

What did the towrope say to the boarder?

"Hey, can I give you a lift?"

Why is the most famous signature board like Lassie?

Because it's a star with a tail!

Why are dogs such bad skaters?

Because they have two left feet—and two right ones!

What game do boarders play when they're bored?

Ride and seek!

Why did the BMXer love his hilarious doctor?

Because she kept him in stitches!

Why is it hard to play cards on a windsurfer?

Because you have to stand on the deck!

Why did the climber think that she was going to be in a movie after her accident?

Because she had to be in the cast right away!

How do lost surfers clean their clothes?

They wash ashore!

How did the biker feel after biking across the archery practice range?

As if he had made an arrow escape!

Why did the climber in the cast feel like an old record?

He was all scratchy!

What did the boarder say to his friend William, who was in his way?

Will, you get out of my way!

What did the chilly boarders sing on New Year's Eve?

"Freeze a jolly good fellow!"

Knock, knock!
Who's there?
Snow!
Snow who?
Snow way I'm going rock climbing—it's too dangerous!

Why did the diver begin her dive in shallow water?

Because she wanted to start on a small scale!

Why did the skater put her board in the freezer?

Because she wanted to chill out her style!

KNOCK, KNOCK!

Knock, knock!
Who's there?
Albany!
Albany who?
Albany of these knock-knock
jokes are there, anyway?

Knock, knock!
Who's there?
Ray!
Ray who?
Ray-member the last time
I was here?

Knock, knock!
Who's there?
Tommy!
Tommy who?
Tommy you'll always be special!

Knock, knock!
Who's there?
Glenda!
Glenda who?
Glenda hand, man,
this is heavy!

Knock, knock!
Who's there?
Dougie!
Dougie who?
Dougie hole in your lawn by
accident! Sorry!

Knock, knock!
Who's there?
Isabel!
Isabel who?
Isabel out of order? I had
to knock!

Knock, knock!
Who's there?
Seek!
Seek who?
Seek-rat agent. That's a seek-rat
I can't tell!

Knock, knock!
Who's there?
Alfred
Alfred who?
Alfred the needle if you'll
tie the knot!

Knock, knock!
Who's there?
Gadget!
Gadget who?
Gadget in your glove or it'll
hit you in the head!

Knock, knock!
Who's there?
Arizona!
Arizona who?
Arizona so many times
I can knock!

Knock, knock!
Who's there?
A. Pierre!
A. Pierre who?
A. Pierre at five o'clock, and
you'll find out!

Knock, knock!
Who's there?
Adolph!
Adolph who?
Adolph ball hit me in
de mowf!

Wacky Wizardry

Why couldn't the cat talk after catching the rodent?

It had a mouse-ful!

⭐🌙⭐

Why did the wizard's cat want to put rodents in the freezer?

It wanted to make mice cubes!

⭐☀️⭐

What did the wizard get when he crossed his hamster with a bodybuilder?

A mouse-el man!

⭐🌙⭐

What did the wizard get when he crossed a rabbit with a rooster?

An ear-ly bird!

What did the wizard get when he crossed a baboon with a tool kit?

A monkey wrench!

⭐🌙⭐

What did the wizard get when he crossed fruit with a math book?

Apple pi!

What did the wizard get when he crossed a liar with some Gouda?

Cheater cheese! (cheddar cheese)

⭐🌙⭐

What did the wizard get when he crossed a snake and a symphony?

A boa conductor!

What did the blackbird say when it took the dinghy across the moat?

"Crow, crow, crow your boat!"

What did the wizard's snake use to eat?

Fork-chops!

☆ ☀ ☆

What did the wizard say when he cast a spell on his snake?

"Abra-da-cobra!"

☆ ☽ ☆

What did the wizard get when he crossed a lizard with the worker who cut his grass?

A gardener snake!

☆ ☀ ☆

What did the wizard get when he crossed a squid with a cat?

An octo-puss!

☆ ☽ ☆

What did the wizard's frog say to the snake?

Hiss me now or lose me forever!

☆ ☀ ☆

What was the snake's favorite subject in school?

Hiss-story!

What did the wizard get when he crossed a vine with a snake?

Poison ivy!

SILLY SPIES

What did the secret agent use to write his autobiography?

Sus-pens! (suspense)

Why did the spy's horse retire?

Because its nerves were shod!

How did the spy feel when he put his hand on the spark plug?

A little shocked!

How did the enemy secret agent like his food?

Scheming hot!

Where did the secret agent catch the dirty crook?

At the scene of the grime!

What do countries call it when they trade agents?

A spy for a spy!

When do villains get read their rights?

When they're in the wrong!

sniff sniff

What did the spy's cat think when it saw the crime scene?

"I smell a rat!"

What do spies call the room where all their long meetings are held?

The bored room!

What did the secret agent think of the magician spy?

That he was tricky!

What do spies call their best basketball squad?

The scheme team!

What did the spy do while he made dinner?

He cooked up a plot!

What did the secret agent say when he caught the slow spy?

"I've uncovered a vicious plod!" (plot)

What did the secret agent say about the suspicious chicken farmer?

"I'll bet he's hatching a plan right now!"

"Plan"

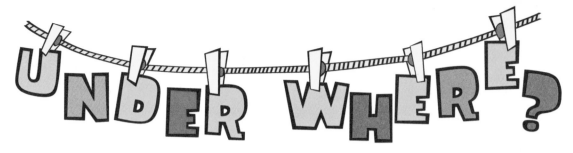

UNDER WHERE?

What do you call underwear that you can't decide whether or not to buy?

Iffy skivvies!

What did they call the monster that ran around in its boxer shorts?

The under-were-wolf!

What did the underwear button say to the hole?

"The eyes have it!"

What do you call a tricky fastener?

A tripper zipper!

How did the man know that his shorts were unhappy?

They got themselves into a real flap!

What do you call long-haired underwear?

Hippies!

How many boxer shorts does it take to make a fruit salad?

Just one pear!

How do you know when your underwear is tired?

When it can't stay up any longer!

Why do you feel so secure in your underwear?

Because you know you're covered!

Why did the man think that his loose underwear was like a pizza?

Because he had to pick them up!

Why is the flap on boxer shorts so attentive?

It sits front and center!

How do you know when it's getting late for your underwear?

When time is running shorts!

What do you say when you see someone's underwear hanging out?

"You look like you're waisting away!"

Why is one sock always missing from the wash?

Because it likes wandering from the laundering!

What do you get when you forget to separate the dark colors from the white boxer shorts?

Blue bottoms!

Knock, knock!
Who's there?
Harlow!
Harlow who?
Harlow do you wear your underpants?

XTREME-LY FUNNY

Why do skateboarders love to go up hills?

To get away from being grounded!

Why are people dumber at the bottom of a chairlift than they are at the top?

Because the crowds are denser down there!

How did the boarder feel when he got toasted on the hill?

He was a little burned up about it!

How did the hard-working skateboarder get such a flat nose?

He kept it to the grindstone!

Why can't army sergeants be good, relaxed surfers?

Because they're always yelling "Ten-sion!"

How did the blind carpenter make such good skateboards?

He just picked up his tools and saw!

Why didn't the windsurfer believe the story about the piranha attack?

Because it sounded fishy!

What happened when a pile of snow fell from a bough onto the boarder's head?

It knocked him out cold!

Why did the big-air jumper come down with a cold?

Because her tricks were just too sick!

What do you get when you cross a snowboard with an ax?

The splits!

What is the worst part about BMX bikes for mice?

The squeaking!

What is the best thing a motocross racer can take when she feels run-down?

The number of the guy who ran over her!

How are pills and hills different?

One is hard to get down and the other is hard to get up!

What did the boarder get when she cut through the treacherous trees?

A short cut!

What did the boarder's dog get?

Trick ticks!

Wacky Wizardry

What did the wizard's frog say
to the toad?

"So, warts on your mind?"

☆ ☾ ☆

What did the wizard get when he crossed
a snowball and a snake?

Frostbite!

☆ ☀ ☆

What did the wizard get when he
crossed a heckler with a parrot?

A mockingbird!

☆ ☾ ☆

What did the wizard say
to the little bird?

Sparrow a moment?

☆ ☀ ☆

What did the wizard get when he
crossed a baseball player
with a chicken?

A fowl ball!

☆ ☾ ☆

What did the wizard get when he
combined a duck and a funny book?

Quacker-jokes!

☆ ☀ ☆

Where did the wizard get his owl?

The stork market!

☆ ☾ ☆

What did the wizard call it when
he pulled a rabbit out of his hat
three times in a row?

A hat trick!

What did the wizard tell the Cyclops who was playing baseball?

"Keep your eye on the ball!"

⭐ ☀️ ⭐

What did the wizard call the bird with an eye patch?

Polly the Pirate!

⭐ 🌙 ⭐

What did the witch get when she crossed a school with a circus?

The class clown!

⭐ ☀️ ⭐

What did the woman say when the wizard told her how much the spell would cost?

"That's a charm and a leg!"

What did the witch get when she crossed a toboggan with some tools?

A sled-hammer!

⭐ 🌙 ⭐

What did the wizard call his spirit friends from Europe?

Portu-ghosts!

⭐ ☀️ ⭐

What did the suit of armor say after being left out in the rain?

"I think I'll lie down for a rust!"

⭐ 🌙 ⭐

What did the suit of armor miss about being worn?

The knight life!

KNOCK, KNOCK!

Knock, knock!
Who's there?
Raymond!
Raymond who?
*Raymond me again
what I'm doing here!*

Knock, knock!
Who's there?
Madge!
Madge who?
*Madge-in my surprise,
you're home!*

Knock, knock!
Who's there?
Sammy!
Sammy who?
*Sammy directions next time, and
I'll get here faster!*

Knock, knock!
Who's there?
Dwight!
Dwight who?
*Dwight when I was gonna
tell you, too!*

Knock, knock!
Who's there?
Greta!
Greta who?
*Greta phone, then I can
stop knocking!*

Knock, knock!
Who's there?
Douglas!
Douglas who?
*Douglas is broken, they must
have come in at night!*

Knock, knock!
Who's there?
Bunny!
Bunny who?
Bunny thing is, I know where the eggs are hidden!

Knock, knock!
Who's there?
Comb!
Comb who?
Comb down and I'll tell you!

Knock, knock!
Who's there?
Eva!
Eva who?
Eva wonder why I always knock?

Knock, knock!
Who's there?
Rabbit!
Rabbit who?
Rabbit around your head like a turban!

Knock, knock!
Who's there?
Ron!
Ron who?
Ron house! Sorry! They all look the same!

Knock, knock!
Who's there?
Roberts!
Roberts who?
Roberts are afraid of alarms!

SILLY SPIES

Why are spies so good
at playing softball?

Because they're underhanded!

What do you call a female spy?

Miss Chevious!

What do evil agents
call their spy classes?

Wick Ed.!

Where did the spy keep his
important fake beards hidden?

In his must-stash!

What did the gumshoe
think of the spy?

That he was a heel!

Why was the detective suspicious
of the Leaning Tower of Pisa?

*Because there was something
crooked about it!*

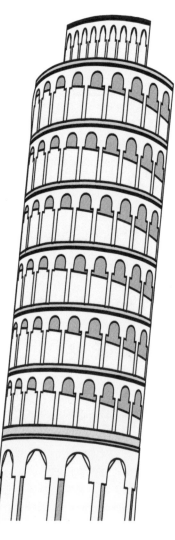

What do mean spies drink?

Nas-tea!

How did the spy get her broken-down stealthmobile home?

She got a tip-tow!

Why didn't the secret agent like the robot spy?

He just couldn't rust him!

What did the spy say about the phone conversation she was tapping?

"This is dial-bolical!"

Why did the enemy's plan make the spy feel sad?

Because it was a blue-print!

Why did the spy hate being underground?

Because everyone else thought he was a lowlife!

What did the enemy spy call his speech about knots?

His tie-rant! (tyrant)

Why did the spy want a green thumb?

So he could plant things on people!

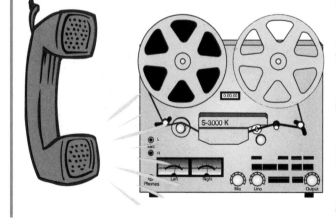

CLASSROOM Crack-ups

What did the student become on his thirteenth birthday?

A teenager!

What is the best way to get by in computer class?

Bit by bit!

Why are math books so hard to get along with?

They have so many problems!

What do you call it when you have to repeat a grade?

Secondary education!

Why are underwater schools so mobile?

Because fish know how to travel in schools!

What did the student say when the teacher accused him of not listening?

"I am listening! I just can't hear you over the snoring!"

What do you call a class in a tree?

High school!

HIGH SCHOOL

What kind of snake is the best at arithmetic?

The adder!

What kind of table has no legs?

The times table!

What did the boy say when he showed up without having his science experiment done?

"My homework ate my dog!"

How difficult is it to be impolite?

It's rude-imentary!

Why did the lowly boy stay home from school?

He had no class!

What do antibiotics and your school desk have in common?

They're both for putting pencil-in! (penicillin)

What kind of plants do math teachers grow?

Ones with square roots!

How did the ghost feel after walking all the way home to the castle?

He was dead on his feet!

☆🌙☆

What did the wizard call the story that the knight told about his horse?

A pony-tail!

☆🌞☆

What did the wizard get when he crossed a cola with a bike?

A pop-cycle!

☆🌙☆

Why did the wizard tell the joke to the ice?

He wanted to see if he could crack it up!

☆🌞☆

What did the wizard call the knight after his clothes shrank?

Tight in shining armor!

☆🌙☆

What did the wizard call the zombie's hair?

Mouldy locks!

What did the witch call the movie she was making about the midnight hour?

A dark-umentary!

☆🌙☆

What did the wizard feed the Italian ghost?

Spook-ghetti!

What did the wizard get when he crossed a frog and a bunny?

A ribbit rabbit!

What did the witch call her popular recipe book?

A best-smeller!

How do witches style their hair?

With scare-spray!

What did the zombie tell the wizard?

"I'm rotten to my friends!"

What did the wizard get when he crossed a banana with a hyena?

Peels (peals) of laughter!

Where did the wizard's daughter find her first boyfriend?

At the Meet Ball!

What did the wizard get when he crossed a scientist with a duck?

A wise-quacker!

Why was the wizard trying to make a legless cow?

To get ground beef!

XTREME-LY FUNNY

What did the cheap racer say when his doctor gave him his bill?

"I thought you said you were going to treat me!"

How did the boarder feel when he fell into a ski jacket face first?

Just a little down in the mouth!

Why were all the fans at the motocross rally wearing white?

Because they were sitting in the bleachers!

How did the boarder think he could get rich by eating Chinese food?

From the fortune cookies!

What did the skier's friends call him after he crashed on his new yellow board?

Banana splits!

What did the boarder say after being late because her bank was robbed?

"Sorry, I got held up!"

Why was the mathematician such a bad surfer in shark-infested waters?

Because he added four and four and got ate!

What did the sign at the ski slope say?

"Laws of Gravity Strictly Enforced!"

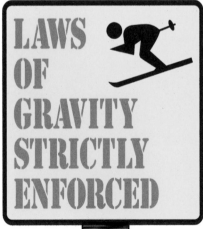

LAWS OF GRAVITY STRICTLY ENFORCED

How did friends calm down the angry sunburned surfer?

They threw water on him so he could let off some steam!

How did the boarder spell "too much air" in just two letters?

X-S!

What do all BMX bikers have in their shoes?

Athlete's feet!

How did the biker feel after she crashed into the pie shop?

A little crusty!

Why do chilled-out boarders hate tennis so much?

They can't stand the racquet!

Why did the skier like the view through his new goggles?

Because he could see from pole to pole!

How did the biker feel when she got a flat in the middle of the race?

A little deflated!

How do big-name skaters stay so cool?

They rely on their fans!

SILLY SPIES

How did the spy see through the suspect's poncho disguise?

He just knew it was a put-on!

Why do detectives need glasses?

Because they get hint squint!

What did Shakespeare call his spy play?

A View to a Quill!

What happened to the spy with bad vision?

He got a sight-ation! (citation)

What did the spy say when asked how he missed seeing the suspect?

"Eye don't know!"

What did scientists try to develop in the lab to help spies?

Smell-o-vision!

Where do spies rest in the middle of a long pursuit?

Chase lounges! (chaise longues)

Why were the spies so quiet while they laid their trap?

Because they were waiting with baited (bated) breath!

How did the detective catch his enemy at the pig farm?

With a ham-bush!

What did the spy say about fishing for clues?

"You really have to lure (lower) your standards!"

What do baby spies play with?

Ploy toys!

What do spies call members of their club?

Their peers!

How did the spy know that he was tired from spying all day?

Because he just couldn't get up the stares!

What did the detective think about the dancing lumberjack case?

It was a real jig-saw puzzle!

KNOCK, KNOCK!

Knock, knock!
Who's there?
Avenue!
Avenue who?
Avenue heard this joke before?

Knock, knock!
Who's there?
Santa!
Santa who?
Santa letter telling you I was coming. Didn't you get it?

Knock, knock!
Who's there?
Moon!
Moon who?
Moon over and let me sit on the couch!

Knock, knock!
Who's there?
Banana!
Banana who?
Knock, knock!
Who's there?
Banana!
Banana who?
Knock, knock!
Who's there?
Banana!
Banana who?
Knock, knock!
Who's there?
Orange!
Orange who?
Orange ya glad I didn't say banana?

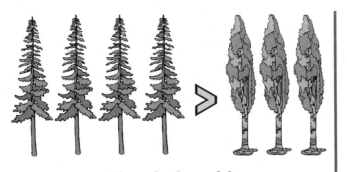

Knock, knock!
Who's there?
Forest!
Forest who?
For-est more than three!

Knock, knock!
Who's there?
Alvin!
Alvin who?
Alvin a nice time on your porch, since you asked!

Knock, knock!
Who's there?
Butcher!
Butcher who?
Butcher money where your mouth is!

Knock, knock!
Who's there?
Tony!
Tony who?
Tony down in there, I'm trying to sleep!

Knock, knock!
Who's there?
Freddy!
Freddy who?
Freddy soon, you're going to find out!

Knock, knock!
Who's there?
Butter!
Butter who?
Butter come inside, it looks like rain!

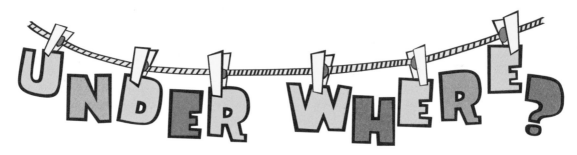

UNDER WHERE?

What do you call the boxer shorts that you wear at the beginning of the week?

Your Monday undies!

Why did the woman throw out her underwear?

Because they had become moldy oldies!

Where do long underwear go to dance?

The moth ball!

What did one moth say to the other when it saw the long underwear?

"Let's eat!"

What do you call underwear that you change into at noon?

A box-ered lunch!

Why weren't the boxer shorts worried about the stinky rumors they had heard?

They figured it would all come out in the wash!

Why are old boxer shorts worried about getting wet?

Because they really have to wash their figure!

Why were the boxer shorts so proud of themselves?

Because they were snug and smug!

What did the silk underwear say about the cotton boxer shorts?

"Pay them no hind!"

Where do boxer shorts for astronauts go?

To underspace!

Knock, knock!
Who's there?
India!
India who?
India morning I always change my underwear!

Why did the man sit on the radiator?

Because he wanted to toast his buns!

What did the boxer shorts say about being ignored?

"Why do you treat me like a bum?"

Why didn't the man mind wearing his flannel boxers on the transatlantic flight?

He liked the idea of being snuggled out of the country!

How did the old boxer shorts feel?

Under appreciated!

What do you think about boxer shorts for rabbits?

They're pretty bunny!

Wacky Wizardry

Why was the wizard's frog
so full and happy?

**Because it ate everything
that bugged it!**

☆ ☽ ☆

What did the wizard get when
he crossed a towel with a frog?

A rubbit!

☆ ☀ ☆

What did the toads in the wizard's swamp
eat when they wanted junk food?

French flies!

Knock, knock!
Who's there?
Ghoul!
Ghoul who?
**Ghoul be sorry if you
don't open up!**

What did the wizard say to
the snake that bit him?

"Fangs a lot!"

☆ ☽ ☆

Old wizard: "Are you sure that your
spell gave your mother eight legs?"

Young wizard: "Sure, I'm sure. I
just spider!"

How did the wizard get his car home
after it broke down?

He toad it!

☆ ☀ ☆

Why do witches come out only
on Halloween?

**Because they're crazy
for candy!**

What did the wizard get
when he crossed a necklace
with an alarm clock?

A diamond ring!

What was the ogre's favorite dish?

Ghoul-ash!

What did the wizard think
of the scary movie?

He thought it was dreadful!

What kind of movies
do witches like best?

Hag-shun films!

What did the wizard get when he crossed
an elephant with a butterfly?

A mam-moth!

Why do wizards wear pointy hats?

*To keep their sharp
minds warm!*

What did the wizard say when he
cast a sleeping spell on his cat?

*"Why don't you paws
for a moment?"*

What did the toad say when
the princess wouldn't kiss him?

"Warts the matter with you?"

SILLY SPIES

Why did the secret agent think the detective was a fake?

Because he was so unreal-lie-able!

What is another name for spyglasses?

Skeptical spectacles!

What do spies call hiding out at night?

Eve-ation! (evasion)

What did the detective say about the double agent climbing the wall?

"I hope he false down on the job!"

What did the spy call his new hat disguise?

His false hood!

What did the secret agent say about the lying spy?

"He has bad moral fibber!"

What did the spy say about the sneaky bear?

"He's so fur-tive!"

What did the spies call the hidden passage that made the rug stick up?

The trip door!

Why did the computer spy quit?

Because he just couldn't hack it anymore!

Blub Blub

Why didn't the spy
trust the car salesman?

*Because she knew that he was a
trader! (traitor)*

What happened when the spy
got caught on the enemy boat?

She was sent up the river!

What do you call a spy
with a couple of disguises?

Two-faced!

Why didn't the spy
trust the whale?

*He knew it was a
blubbermouth!*

What did the spies
call their female boss?

Miss Chief! (mischief)

XTREME-LY FUNNY

Why did the BMXer wish that her coach was on the radio?

Because then she could have turned him off!

Why wasn't the boarder worried about the icy patches on the pipe?

He thought that they were skid stuff!

How can a skier jump off a giant mountain and not get hurt?

She can wait until she gets to the bottom!

How did the surfer fix his banana board?

With a monkey wrench!

What time was it when the climbers came across the bear?

Time to run!

Should a surfer ever swim on a full stomach?

No, he should swim on the ocean!

Why did the wimpy racer love to send mail?

She knew that she could at least lick the stamps!

Why did the skier refuse to race against any jungle cats?

Because they were all cheetahs!

What did the boarder think when he saw his picture hanging in a window?

He thought he'd been framed!

Why did the skaters stop hanging out with their slingshot-crazy pal?

He was always shooting his mouth off!

How did the boarder feel when her friend skied right over her?

A little run-down!

Knock, knock!
Who's there?
Doughnut!
Doughnut who?
Doughnut forget to wear a helmet!

What did the climber say to his jacket before he went into a cave?

"Cover me, I'm going in!"

What did the boarder say after nearly cutting herself chopping wood?

"That was almost an ax-ident!"

What do BMXers call police officers assigned to the races?

Cop cycles!

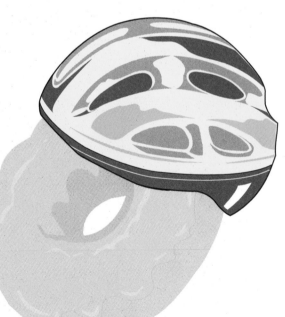

KNOCK, KNOCK!

Knock, knock!
Who's there?
Evans!
Evans who?
Evans to Betsy, you look tired!

Knock, knock!
Who's there?
Berlin!
Berlin who?
Berlin hot out here,
ain't it?

Knock, knock!
Who's there?
Moscow!
Moscow who?
Moscows moo but this one
seems very quiet!

Knock, knock!
Who's there?
Boston!
Boston who?
Boston left me in charge of the
office for the day!

Knock, knock!
Who's there?
Kansas!
Kansas who?
Kansas what tuna
comes in!

Knock, knock!
Who's there?
L.A.!
L.A. who?
L.A. down to take a nap and
I slept right through dinner!

Knock, knock!
Who's there?
Gertie!
Gertie who?
Gertie dishes are no fun!

Knock, knock!
Who's there?
May!
May who?
May my bed for me, would you?

Knock, knock!
Who's there?
Myron!
Myron who?
Myron is clean! Honest!

Knock, knock!
Who's there?
Gladys!
Gladys who?
Gladys finally Friday. I can't take another day of school!

Knock, knock!
Who's there?
Sadie!
Sadie who?
Sadie magic words, and I'll tell you!

Knock, knock!
Who's there?
Ida!
Ida who?
Ida done my homework if my dog hadn't eaten it!

Wacky Wizardry

What did the wizard say about
working with animals?

"It's aard-vark!"

☆ ☀ ☆

What did the wizard get when he
crossed a potato with a priest?

A chip-monk!

☆ ☽ ☆

What do wizards do
before they go to bed?

They spell their prayers!

☆ ☀ ☆

What did the wizard call the necklace
made out of lettuce?

Salad gold!

☆ ☽ ☆

What did the wizard get when he crossed
a movie star with a monster?

E-lizard-Beth Taylor!

☆ ☀ ☆

What did the wizard call
a resting place for birds?

A cemet-airy!

☆ ☽ ☆

What did the wizard call his surly servant?

Stormy waiter!

☆ ☀ ☆

How do wizards remember?

They visit Memory Lane!

☆ ☽ ☆

What did the wizard
call the monster that wore a robe?

The Kimono (Komodo) dragon!

What did the wizard say
about the shy witch?

"Oh, she's just bats-full!"

Why did the wizard love to
tell jokes to his owl?

*Because the owl always
gave a hoot!*

Which singer do
astronomer wizards like best?

Ricky Martian!

Why did the monster's guitar
sound better after being in
the basement for a long time?

*Because it had
been tombed! (tuned)*

What instrument does a wizard
on vacation play?

The Bermuda Triangle!

Where do wizards
get their honey?

From spelling bees!

UNDER WHERE?

What did the old man say about his favorite shorts?

"I love my goody two shorts!"

How did the woman feel about her low-rise underwear?

She thought they were pretty hip!

Why did the two legs of the long johns want to stay together?

They were an old couple!

What did the man wear under his suit at the luncheon?

His tea shirt!

What do you call someone who loves to look for underwear?

Short-sighted!

What do you call bright silk briefs?

Shiny tinies!

How did the long johns know that they were going to be shortened?

They saw it coming at the cut-off!

Knock, knock!
Who's there?
Kenya!
Kenya who?
Kenya guess what color my underwear is?

What do you call boxers that are too big?

Roomy bloomers!

How did the captain feel about going down with the ship in his underwear?

He had a shrinking feeling!

What did the underwear call the big, dim-witted man who wore them?

A simple-ton!

Why did the Neanderthal suddenly start wearing underwear?

One day, he just caved!

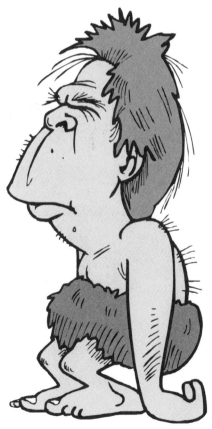

What kind of shorts did dinosaurs wear?

Bronto boxers!

What do you call shorts held up with ivory?

Waist-boned!

How did the man feel about getting his shorts caught on the door handle?

He was a little hung up about it!

261

KNOCK, KNOCK!

Knock, knock!
Who's there?
Gorilla!
Gorilla who?
Gorilla cheese is good
with ketchup!

Knock, knock!
Who's there?
Eggs!
Eggs who?
Eggs-men are everywhere!

Knock, knock!
Who's there?
Olive!
Olive who?
Olive the times I've been
to your house and you
still don't recognize me?

Knock, knock!
Who's there?
Grape!
Grape who?
Grape game the other day.
You're still the champ!

Knock, knock!
Who's there?
Stan!
Stan who?
Stan back, or I'll kick the
door down!

Knock, knock!
Who's there?
Pizza!
Pizza who?
Pizza me! I'm as surprised
as you are!

Knock, knock!
Who's there?
Sonny!
Sonny who?
Sonny side up please!

Knock, knock!
Who's there?
Ooze!
Ooze who?
Ooze the boss around
here, anyway?

Knock, knock!
Who's there?
Shoe!
Shoe who!
Shoe kid, you're bothering me!

Knock, knock!
Who's there?
Julia!
Julia who?
Julia think I'm gonna tell you?

Knock, knock!
Who's there?
Wylie!
Wylie who?
Wylie answers the door, the
bathtub is overflowing!

Knock, knock!
Who's there?
Caesar!
Caesar who?
Caesar before she has time
to fill up her squirt gun!

TEACHER TICKLERS

What did the student say when the teacher reminded her that she'd had detention every day?

"Thank heaven it's Friday!"

What did the student say when the teacher asked why he didn't know any answers?

"If I did, why would I come to class?"

Teacher: "Which month has 28 days?"

Student: "All of 'em!"

Teacher: "I told you to go to the back of the line!"

Student: "I did, but someone was already there!"

Teacher: "Please recite the longest sentence!"

Student: "Twenty-five to life!"

What do you call a teacher who can see with her back turned?

Four-eyes!

What did the students call the teacher who threw surprise tests?

Pops!

Teacher: "Why were things better in 1900 than now?"

Student: "There was less history to learn!"

Teacher: "How can you get so many wrong answers in one day?"

Student: "I start very early!"

What did the student say when the teacher asked where elephants are found?

"You lost an elephant?"

Why should the two chemistry teachers have known better than to date?

They should have seen the science! (signs)

Teacher: "What do you get when you divide 608 by 53?"

Student: "The wrong answer!"

Teacher: "Today we're going to try something different!"

Student: "What's that?"

Teacher: "Learning!"

Teacher: "What proof do you have that the world is round?"

Student: "I didn't say it was, you did! You prove it!"

What is worse than a teacher finding a worm in her apple?

Finding half a worm!

265

XTREME-LY FUNNY

How did the cheap boarder
work out in the off-season?

By pinching pennies!

What did the boarder's dog have
to keep it warm?

A fleas (fleece) coat!

Why did the skier get
frostbite on his legs?

*Because he couldn't figure out how
to get pants on over his skis!*

Why do boarders hate
doing laundry in the winter?

*They're afraid of
ring around the colder! (collar)*

Why did the boarder buy
his dog a fur coat?

*Because he didn't want it
to be a little bear! (bare)*

Why did the skater think that she
could glide across the country?

*Because she had heard about a
coast-to-coast trip!*

*Knock, knock!
Who's there?
Bailey!
Bailey who?
Bailey me out of the snow!*

How did the figure skater know
that her skates were tired?

*Because their tongues
were hanging out!*

How did the surfer feel after too much coffee?

Really perky!

How do boarders make their snowpants last?

They put on their jackets first!

How does a boarder make his bed longer?

He adds his two feet to it!

What did the boarder call the person who stole his dog?

A spot remover!

What did the motocross racer say after she crossed the dirty finish?

Oh, don't give me that old line!

What is bright red and has a trunk?

A burned surfer heading home from vacation!

What did the skateboarder sing when he saw a cow at the top of the half-pipe?

"The hills are alive with the sound of mooing!"

Moooo

Wacky Wizardry

What did the wizard
tell the movie star?

**"I think you've got
a fan to see!" (fantasy)**

☆🌙☆

What did the wizard call the monster
that ate its brother?

A munch-kin!

☆☀☆

What did the wizard get when he
crossed a monarch with a snake?

A king cobra!

☆🌙☆

What did the wizard use
to catch a fish for dinner?

Hali-bait!

☆☀☆

What kind of car do
creepy-crawly witches drive?

Beetles!

☆🌙☆

What did the wizard
call the knight with no home?

The bedless horseman!

☆☀☆

What did the wizard call the little
gourds that he had grown?

Pumpkin-bred!

☆🌙☆

What did the wizard say
to the witty ogre?

**"You've got a troll
sense of humor!"**

What do you call witches
who work in hospitals?

Health scare!

☆ ☀ ☆

What did the wizard get when
he crossed a pumpkin with a plant?

A jack-o'-lan-fern!

☆ ☽ ☆

What did the wizard call the cloak
that he had made out of fish?

A cape cod!

☆ ☀ ☆

What did the wizard say about
his wife's longest spell?

"She was in a cast for weeks!"

What did the wizard call the twin ghosts?

A-pair-itions!

☆ ☀ ☆

What did the wizard make his crazy
friend for dessert?

Upside-down kook!

☆ ☽ ☆

What do you call 12-dozen worms
on a wizard's counter?

Gross!

☆ ☀ ☆

When do ghosts graduate?

When they have the fright stuff!

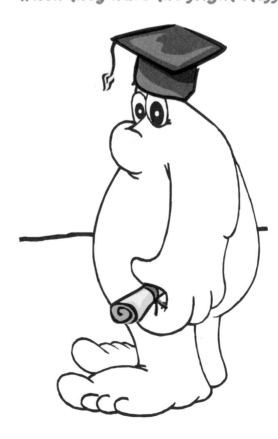

KNOCK, KNOCK!

Knock, knock!
Who's there?
Dill!
Dill who?
Dill we meet again, my sweet!

Knock, knock!
Who's there?
Norma Lee!
Norma Lee who?
Norma Lee I wouldn't come over this late, but can I borrow some milk?

Knock, knock!
Who's there?
Canvas!
Canvas who?
Canvas be true?

Knock, knock!
Who's there?
Earl!
Earl who?
Earl gladly tell you if you'd open up!

Knock, knock!
Who's there?
Bat!
Bat who?
Bat you can't wait to find out!

Knock, knock!
Who's there?
Cherry!
Cherry who?
Cherry this for me, will you? My back's killing me!

Knock, knock!
Who's there?
Terry!
Terry who?
Terry what, why don't you lend me a dollar?

Knock, knock!
Who's there?
Epstein!
Epstein who?
Epstein some crazy people, but you take the cake!

Knock, knock!
Who's there?
Sparrow!
Sparrow who?
Sparrow couple of quarters, pal?

Knock, knock!
Who's there?
Lark!
Lark who?
Lark I'm going to tell you!

Knock, knock!
Who's there?
Goose!
Goose who?
Goose the doctor, you look sick!

SILLY SPIES

What did the spy call his
mother's sister?

The auntie hero!

What do you call a spy
who leaves the dinner table early?

A dessert-er!

What did the secret agents
call the spy who was
dim-witted in court?

The evi-dunce!

What do spies say to their children
when they are naughty?

"You are under-grounded!"

What did the secret agent
say about the small magician
who picked pockets?

"He's light of hand!"
(sleight of hand)

What did the detective say when
someone tried to hand him a phone?

"Just the fax, ma'am!"

Why did the ghost spy
love his job?

*Because he just couldn't phantom
(fathom) doing anything else!*

What happened between
the two opposing agents
at the butcher shop?

Ham-to-ham combat!

Why did the spy call the
pat of butter cowardly?

Because it was yellow!

Why was the spy afraid
of telephones?

It was just one of her hang-ups!

How could the spy hear secrets
in the swimming pool?

He knew how to read laps!

Why did the spy have to
take a sick day?

*Because she had
strained her ears!*

Why did the spy have a
cast on his ear?

*Because he had heard
a broken code!*

What did the spy say when he
couldn't find his magician son?

"I lose son!"
(illusion)

Why did the old-time surfer
think he could get his hair
cut at sea?

*He thought he saw a
clipper ship!*

What did the biker think about
crashing into the wall?

It cracked her up!

What did the young guys
call the old surfer who
stood around all day?

The dust collector!

How did the boarder feel when
he crashed into the baker?

A little crumby!

Why didn't the skater trust
her new shoes?

*Because she thought they
were sneakers!*

What did the surfer think of the
dentist who fixed his teeth?

He thought she was boring!

What did the skater think of
the man who fixed her shoes?

She thought he was a heel!

How did the biker feel
about the race after
his tire popped?

He felt like he'd blown it!

What did the skaters think of the blue-haired boarder with the big shoes?

They thought he was a clown!

Why did the boarder wear a cabbage on her helmet?

Because she wanted to get a-head!

Why did the skater throw his Airwalks into the competition bowl?

Because he wanted to be a shoe-in!

How did the hang glider feel when he crashed into the garbage?

A little down in the dumps!

What did the diver call the fish doctor?

A brain sturgeon!

How do late-night bike races start?

"On your mark, get set, glow!"

What did the boarder think of the pinecones that the squirrels dropped on him?

He thought they were nuts!

275

What did the wizard call the psychic who kept growing?

Fortune Taller!

What did the wizard call the monster named Theodore?

Demon-Ted! (demented)

What did the rabbit say to the sorcerer?

"Wiz up, doc?"

What did the wizard say after his wife starting throwing dishes?

"Look out! Flying saucers!"

What did the wizard get when he crossed a planet with a dish?

The World Cup!

What do wizards like about alphabet soup?

They can spell while they eat!

What did the wizard call the knight's naughty horse?

A night mare!

What did the wizard's wife say when he bought her a new cloak?

"Oh, you're so robe-mantic!"

What did the wizard get when he crossed a writing tool with a bird?

A pen-guin!

What did the wizard call the scales he dug up in the backyard?

Buried measure!

What did the wizard call the dog after he had shrunk it?

Spot!

What did the wizard say when his pen exploded?

"I've got that inking feeling again!"

What did the wizard call the jewelry that he gave to his wife?

Married treasure!

How do you know if a wizard is happy?

He's going through a smiling spell!

What do you call a strange hairy wizard?

A beardo!

What did the witch call the wizard with no hair?

Baldy locks!

What is the best way to get into the whole topic of underwear?

One foot at a time!

What did the man think about his new underwear's waistband?

He thought it was pretty snappy!

What did the man think about his unraveling underwear?

He thought that it had lost the thread somewhere!

Knock, knock!
Who's there?
Abel!
Abel who?
I'm Abel to see your underwear!

What did the sock think about the stuffy underwear?

It thought that it was a little full of itself!

What do you call the most comfy socks around?

Cozy toesies!

Why was the underwear so sad?

Because it was bummed out!

How do you feel when you put on a new pair of boxers?

Short changed!

In what area does your underwear like to hang out?

Near the rear!

What kind of underwear did the big old elephant wear?

Woolly mammoths!

Did it take long for the new underwear styles to become popular?

No, they really cott-on quickly!

Why should suspenders be arrested?

For holding up your shorts!

What did the boxer shorts say to the stockings that were hanging out to dry?

"Oh, don't give me that old line!"

Knock, knock!
Who's there!
Gertie!
Gertie who?
Gertie underwear goes in the hamper!

What did the reader think of the boxer-shorts jokes?

They wore him out!

What do you call a playwright who goes on and on about stockings?

Sockspeare!

Pet Punchlines

Where did the pet bird invest its time?

In the stork market!

Which martial art do ninja budgies practice?

Kung flew!

Why did the parakeet go dutch on dates?

Because he was cheep!

What kind of bird gulps the loudest?

The swallow!

Why are owls so much fun as pets?

Because they're a real hoot to be around!

Why did the little old lady want to get rid of her pet bird?

Because it used fowl language!

When is a dog like a person catching a cold?

When it's a little husky!

Why did the parrot cross the road?

To prove that it wasn't a chicken!

What do you call a chicken that makes funny yolks?

A comedi-hen!

Boy: **Why don't you believe that I have a pet rat?**

Girl: *"Because you're always telling tails!"*

Why don't flying mice make good pets?

Bats me!

What kind of cat sounds happiest?

A Purrrrsian! (Persian)

What do you say to your pet after it has finished eating its pellets?

"Here's gerbil (your bill), sir. I hope you enjoyed your meal!"

What do you say when you want your pet python to sing with you?

"Let's wrap!" (rap)

KNOCK, KNOCK!

Knock, knock!
Who's there?
Candice!
Candice who?
Candice be any better!

Knock, knock!
Who's there?
Hardy!
Hardy who?
Hardy recognized you without
my glasses on!

Knock, knock!
Who's there?
Mice!
Mice who?
Mice to make
your acquaintance!

Knock, knock!
Who's there?
Pitcher!
Pitcher who?
Pitcher eye up to the window
and see for yourself!

Who's there?
Cows go!
Cows go who?
No, they don't! Cows go moo!

Knock, knock!
Who's there?
Ammonia!
Ammonia who?
Ammonia little kid!

Here I am.

Knock, knock!
Who's there?
Beaver!
Beaver who?
Beaver quiet and nobody
will find us!

Knock, knock!
Who's there?
Rat!
Rat who?
Rat seems to be the problem?

Knock, knock!
Who's there?
Howzer!
Howzer who?
Howzer day going?

Knock, knock!
Who's there?
Jason!
Jason who?
Jason you all day is
making me tired!

Knock, knock!
Who's there?
Dogs!
Dogs who?
No, they don't! Owls hoot!

WHOOO!

283

What did the diver overhear one fish saying to another?

"One of these days, you'll get caught with your mouth open!"

How did the hungry surfer feel after she'd swallowed some salt water?

It just whet her appetite!

What did the biker say to the horse?

"Hey, why the long face?"

What did the boarders call the longest snowball fight?

The Cold War!

What did the muscle-building biker say when he couldn't get a ring out of his bike?

"Dumb bell!"

What did everyone call the miserly skater who was always wiping out?

Cheapskate!

What do you call the supporters who are first up the hill?

Chair leaders!

How did the diver try to communicate with the big fish?

She thought she would drop it a line!

How did the biker feel after he crashed into the turkey truck?

Pretty stuffed!

Why don't felines surf?

Because they prefer cat-amarans!

What did the boarders call the skeleton who tried to board?

Gutless!

Why are mountain climbers so bad at Christmas?

They just can't resist a peak!

Did you hear about the boarder's fashion crime?

He used a pair of suspenders to hold up his pants!

Why was the poor boarder's dog always chasing its tail?

It was trying to make ends meet!

What did the skater say to the curb?

"I don't want any of your lip!"

What did the boarder's cat hate most about walking home after a rainstorm?

The poodles!

What did the witch offer guests who stayed at her house?

Broom and board!

☆ ☽ ☆

What do ghouls call their loudest member?

Their spooksman!

☆ ☀ ☆

What do witches like to give children for dessert?

Eye scream!

Why was the wizard upset to learn that his spiders were married?

Because he hadn't been invited to the webbing!

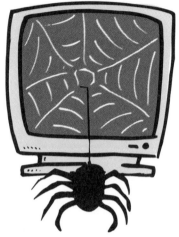

What did the spider say to the fly in the wizard's castle?

"Welcome to my Web site!"

☆ ☽ ☆

Why was the wizard so excited to get his new spiders home?

He wanted to take them out for a spin!

☆ ☀ ☆

What did the fly call the spider's lair?

A lethal webbin'! (weapon)

☆ ☽ ☆

What did the witch need when her sewing machine got broken?

A spin doctor!